You Are Here On the Earth to Enjoy Everything
The New Teaching of God

G000123459

Daniel Neusom

To order additional copies, please contact us.
BookSurge, LLC
www.booksurge.com
1-866-308-6235
orders@booksurge.com

You Are Here On the Earth to Enjoy Everything

Table of Contents

Acknowledgements

Every person whose life has touched mine has assisted me on my journey home.

I will always be grateful to my spiritual teacher Ann White for saving my life and facilitating my opening to God.

Thank you Christian Bain for so generously giving your time, energy, and editorial gifts to bring this book together.

Thank you Julie Berndt and Rev. Catherine Brooks for your contributions to this project and to my ministry.

Thank you Arlene Gottfried for creating the cover photo which so beautifully personifies the content and teachings of this book.

Thank you Reverands Jim Webb, George Brooks, Valerie Lynn-Logue, Lyn Skreczko Van Riper and Miriam Kangiwa, Dr. Elisabeth Macrae, Dolores Ellner and Jennifer Sage for your love, support and spiritual gifts which are a source of daily sustenance in my life.

Thank you Mark Wren and Charlene Rouson for creating my television ministry and offering your gifts in service to God.

A special thanks to Hawa Shehu and James Brennan for all you have given and continue to give me.

To all of the members and friends of The Sacred Light Fellowship, to every student and client I have been privileged to serve, Thank you!! Without your presence and desire to open and grow I could not receive the amazing teachings which come through my channel, and this book would not exist.

About the Author

Rev. Neusom works as channel, spiritual psychotherapist, lecturer, pastor and spiritual teacher. He is also an award-winning singer-songwriter and flutist.

Rev. Neusom's previous channeled work, the life-changing book, *On Earth as it is in Heaven*, was published in 1999. He lives in Brooklyn, New York and can be reached through his website www.danielneusom.com.

Introduction

Many people who have read my previous book, *On Earth as it is in Heaven,* have asked when my next book is coming out. It's wonderful to know that *On Earth as it is in Heaven* has been such a life-changing experience for so many people who've read it. Spirit has now guided me in the creation of a new book.

Twenty-three years ago after a suicide attempt, I called out to God and asked for healing and help. I had hit rock bottom. Rock bottom was a powerful place for me to be because it gave me the humility to be taught and transformed by the Spirit of God. Spirit guided me to my earthly spiritual teacher, Ann White, who guided me through a deep path of spiritual psychotherapy.

At that time I just wanted to make it through a day; little did I know that it is possible to live in heaven on earth. Heaven is a state of consciousness where you are no longer in conflict with yourself and love yourself unconditionally, where you are no longer angry and hurt over the past, where you no longer have or believe in guilt, and you know and accept that you are always innocent. Because consciousness creates and manifests reality, when you are in the consciousness of heaven, your outer life manifests in overflowing abundance and fulfillment in every way and on every level.

Does this sound like an impossible dream that's too good to be true? I thought so until I unexpectedly reached the consciousness of heaven and started experiencing it as my physical life. This occurred after seven years of intense spiritual psychotherapeutic work on my self, guided at first by my earthly spiritual teacher. My meditation and healing work with her in turn opened me to my angelic guides in the realm of spirit.

There are Angelic beings who guide the spiritual path of humanity. When any person truly chooses to heal and transform, God sends angels to guide their way.

I'm sure you have said or heard *The Lord's Prayer*. When Jesus says "Thy kingdom come, thy will be done on earth as it is in Heaven," he's not kidding.

For those readers who are new to my ministry, I would like to explain how I work. As mentioned above, my spiritual practice opened me to direct communication with heavenly spiritual teachers. When I move into a meditative state, I'm able to hear the voice of Spirit through my own consciousness.

This hearing is telepathic. It began as a quiet voice, which through years of practice has become a distinctive voice of the Holy Spirit of God and of the angels of Healing and Transformation—the Holy Spirit of God and the angelic realm communicating love and healing through my body and energy field.

Although most of this book comes to you directly from Spirit, I have added my own comments as I am guided to do so. The message that follows is my prayer that you be released from all pain, suffering, struggle and lack, and to help you open to the consciousness and experience of Heaven on earth.

Rev. Daniel B. Neusom, New York, August 2005

To all of humanity as we open to healing and higher consciousness, to The Creator of All Life Everywhere, and to the Great Arc Angels who serve God's Light.
I also dedicate this book to my beloved friend Fred Morris whose love on the Earth has opened and transformed me.

Part 1

The Holy Spirit of God

Be Still and Know that I am God

I am communicating with you and loving you whenever I find openings in you where you can receive Me.

In truth We are one, so when you call for Me I must respond. You are very afraid now—in fact you are in crisis—so I am reaching you whenever there is any opening.

Be still and know that I am God. I ask you now to breathe in that truth as I assure you that in reality you have nothing to fear.

If in your life right now you are experiencing crisis or upheaval, or you are afraid of experiencing crisis and upheaval in the future, please know that is part of your Self calling out, crying out for healing, and that I am the healing you seek.

I am your God, your Creator, and I live within you and around you. You live and move and have your being within Me and I am love.

Be still and know that I am love. I am the love that gave you life. When you ask Me to heal you and help you, I will, I *must,* because We are one. I am within you and you are within Me.

When you ask Me to heal you and help you, I will: *I must because We are one*. I am within you and you are within Me.

There are parts of you that have been separated from Me for eons of time. Those parts of you do not know Me or trust Me.

These are parts of you that have never known love, parts of your Self that you have never loved. I am calling you now to love yourself with all your Heart, all of your Soul, all of your Mind, with all that you are.

Prayer is the process by which you open to My Spirit within you and give Me permission to love you into wholeness and freedom. In this book I will teach you how to pray effectively.

Effective prayer places My light at the causal level of your experiences. Effective prayer gives Me permission to transform your consciousness.

When I speak of your consciousness I am speaking of your thoughts, feelings, beliefs and perceptions. Your beliefs are caused by what you perceive and what you think about what you perceive. Your feelings respond to what you have experienced, which was created by your thoughts, feelings, beliefs and perceptions.

My son Michael is working with you now on the level of feeling in the emotional body, which you experience in your physical body in the solar plexus, the gut. Your emotional body is awesomely powerful. It magnetically draws into manifestation what you physically experience as your life.

Often your thoughts and feelings are not in agreement with each other. It is easy to intellectually receive and take in new information, but not so easy to emotionally integrate it. This is why I am guiding humanity into more and more emotional release.

Emotional release frees you of old emotional imprinting that lives in your emotional body so that you become free to receive new life, new light. Allowing yourself to receive Me in truth as you release emotionally literally frees you, frees your Soul of the imprinting that creates your suffering, struggle and lack.

Behold I make all things new.

I will describe My vision for you, My vision of humanity. According to My will, My vision, you love your Self fully, passionately, unconditionally, with all of your Heart, Soul, mind, and being—with all you are.

Your entire being is filled with this love, which is My presence. You are completely filled with My presence. So within you there is no room for guilt, or self-judgment, or old emotional imprinting.

You are fully in the present and you are unafraid of life because you know there is nothing within you that has the possibility of creating pain for you. So you feel and know and live as if there is nothing to fear, and there isn't.

If you do not understand anything I'm communicating with you through this channel, please pause and go within and ask Me to make it clearer to you—and *breathe*...

All of the understandings will open within you eventually.

I am describing to you now the fact that you literally create what you experience with your thoughts, feelings, beliefs and perceptions. When there is no unhealed emotional imprinting within, when you no longer believe in guilt, or judge yourself for anything in any way, you cannot and will not create pain for yourself.

You *can* then live fearlessly—fulfilling your purpose of enjoying everything and expanding Our light through your fulfilled and joyous life.

❧

Arc Angel Michael brought a teaching through this channel, which I will now bring forward. Your judgment of Self creates blocks in your life. Your acceptance of self opens you to receive.

Please work often with this prayer, this affirmation of truth:

I will not judge myself for anything in any way.

Your judgments of yourself create a strong "No" current, which blocks you from receiving all of the gifts of love that I am always sending to you. Your total acceptance of Self—of everything you say, do, think, feel, and experience and everything you have thought, felt, said, believed and experienced—leaves you always open to receiving all that I am and all that I am always giving to you. Praise God!

I want you to really reflect on what We have just given you. There is never a reason for you to judge yourself for anything in any way. Breathe that in. Reflect on it.

Now let's look at the fact that you have been judging yourself for everything all of the time. And if you are honest with yourself, you always fall short in your own judgment. There is a direct correlation between your judgments of self and your happiness, peace, joy and fulfillment.

An inner judge has taken form in your psyche. This judge is constantly evaluating and grading you. For some of you this is the voice of your parents and especially the parent you felt most unloved and unseen by.

For the more religiously oriented this is an image of Me — a perfect God whom you have sinned against who has cast you out of heaven, outside of his love and whom you can never please. Listen closely and you may hear yourself say: "If only I were perfect I would deserve God's mercy and love. If only I were perfect, then I would be worthy of being loved and would be loved. If I were good enough and loving enough and on and on".

Relax, angel of God. You are our beloved child in whom We are always so well pleased. You do not have to be anything other than who and what you are in order to be fully worthy of receiving all of our gifts and all of our love.

The entire creation belongs to you and is your due. All that We have is yours. All that We are is yours. You have no sin. You have nothing to atone for. You have no karmic debts to pay. There is no price you ever have to pay for your life. In truth, you are free right here and right now.

I am speaking to you now — this is My word. I love you unconditionally. Feel and experience My love as you read these words. Receive Me. Receive Me. Receive Me.

While you read this book you may need to pause and take in the Light that I am sending you. I have opened you and you can ask Me any question about what you are reading and I will answer you. Beloved of My Heart, I am the love, which gave you life, and life is My will for you: life, with no suffering, struggle, sacrifice and lack. In the teaching We have given to the earth through the spirit of Jesus, *A Course in Miracles*, We tell you that when you find no value in sickness you will let it go.

I ask you to ask yourself: what is the value of suffering, struggle and lack?

What purpose do suffering, struggle, sacrifice and lack serve for you? Meditate deeply on this with Me.

Suffering, struggle and lack are not My will for you. You do not need them to grow or to become enlightened. I am encouraging you to work on this in our ongoing dialogue and meditation.

Suffering, struggle, sacrifice and lack are serving no purpose in my life. I release them now from My mind, from My body, from My energy field, and from My life. Thank you, God.

I guide you to work with this prayer daily, breathing light in after each time you say it. Say it three times in succession, pausing after each time to breathe Me in. Praise God.

It is so important for you to create a time to receive Me each day to process your life and receive your daily bread from My Heart.

In the Lord's Prayer given to you by your elder Brother Jesus, the words "Give us this day our daily bread" also have a deeper meaning, referring to the process of receiving Me as Light (spiritual energy) as well as the process of receiving My guidance as teachings to help you to live successfully.

As you read these words, I want you to feel My presence within and around you and to know Me as the love, which gave you life, and as the spirit within you who is always saying "Yes" to you.

Feel the truth that I in no way judge you or want you to struggle, suffer or experience lack of any kind in any way. My desire for you is that you open to and experience heaven on earth, right here and right now. Hallelujah!!

Homecoming

In previous teachings through this channel I have spoken of the false ego. The false ego is the part of you that insists on saying No to you when I am saying Yes.

Most of you have chosen not to own this part of yourself, so it remains unconscious to you. The false ego is creating for you everything you experience that you consciously do not want to experience. Praise God!!

This would be a good time for you to pause and breathe in My Light. Allow it to fill you completely and make all things new within and around you and say the following prayer:

There is a part of me creating everything I consciously don't want to be experiencing. Father/Mother God, help me to know that part of myself so that I can realize my power and my false ego can be healed and transformed.

Beloved of God, if you will consistently bring this prayer to Me in meditation I will bring your false ego into complete consciousness and We will transform it so that you can live in heaven on earth.

This would be a good time for you to pause and breathe in My Light. Allow it to fill you completely and make all things new within and round you.

Now what are we doing? Why am I speaking to you through this book? Because, My angel, you have let Me know that you are ready to come home. Being ready to come home does not mean being ready to die and go to heaven. It means you are ready to accept and receive Me as your center and live forever more in heaven as you walk the earth and in any dimension you are drawn to, embodied or unembodied. Praise God.

The purpose of these teachings, the purpose of meditation, the purpose of prayer, the purpose of affirmation, the purpose of emotional release is to make you vibrationally compatible with Me, with My light, so that you no longer suffer, struggle, or experience lack of any kind in any way.

Prayer

Prayer is the conscious act of saying "Yes" to My spirit within you, which is in reality saying "Yes" to your self. Praise God!

On the earth you choose to live under the guidance and control of your human ego self, and so you do not experience the miraculous. You are controlled by the consciousness of fear and lack and you experience the manifestations of this consciousness of fear and lack: illness, loss, loneliness, poverty and death.

You have actually chosen to experience that life in order to learn what you want and need to learn from the experience. When you pray, you are calling forth love—not the ego s love but Divine love!

The ego's love is possessive, controlling, domineering and quite conditional. It says: I love you as long as you behave in accordance with my agenda.

Divine love is miraculous, creative, unconditional and healing. Divine Love is literally the love, which gave you life. Hallelujah!!

My purpose in offering this book through this channel is to give you an experience of Me in reality. When you call Me and hold an image of the Biblical God, you will not be open to receive Me in fullness and reality.

I am the love, which gave you life. I am within you at your center. I am always saying "Yes" to you. It is impossible for Me to ever say "No" to you because I am "Yes". Praise God.

I never judge you or deny you or withhold from you. I am the love which gave you life. And as the love which gave you life, I want you to have life, if that is your choice.

For a long time—for all of the lives you have lived on the earth—you have believed that I am something that I am not. When you are reborn in a new incarnation, you pick up or inherit the consciousness prevalent on the earth. You absorb the psychic imagery and imprinting.

I am here on the earth, present, as I have never been before in this era. I am breaking through all of the lies and illusions you have believed in. You have no sin. You have nothing to atone for. You have no karmic debts to pay. There is no price you ever have to pay for your life and to be in heaven.

Here is a prayer I want you to work with frequently:

I have no sin. I have nothing to atone for. There is no price I ever have to pay for my life of heaven on earth. Thank you, God.

As you work with this prayer and breathe Me in We will dissolve the lies and illusions in your consciousness and you will experience your freedom. You will experience Me making all things new within you and this will manifest as all things being made new around you. Thank you, God.

You can ask Me for anything and everything in prayer and I will always answer you. However, if you don t feel deserving of receiving what you are asking for, or if you are afraid of receiving what you are asking for, it will not manifest.

This does not mean that I have not heard you or am not answering you. It means you are blocked to receiving that which you are asking for and I must unblock you first before you can receive.

I unblock you through emotional release and through teaching you the truth of My unconditional love for you and acceptance of all that you are. I will teach you about emotional release in our next chapter.

So we will focus now on prayers to move you into a consciousness of deservingness. Praise God. As My holy beloved child, your deservingness is without limit, without question and absolutely and utterly unalterable. Nothing can ever or will ever change the fact of your unlimited deservingness.

You can believe otherwise. You can believe and feel that you are undeserving. But just because you believe, and feel it, does not make it true.

I am communicating to you in this book to tell you the truth. As My child your deservingness is always unlimited, no matter what you say or what you have said, do or have done, think and have thought, feel and have felt, experience or have experienced. Praise God.

I ask you to work frequently with the following prayer:

As the child of God my deservingness is unlimited. I am now and forever more in a consciousness of unlimited deservingness. Thank you, God.

Breathe that in and repeat it three times, pausing each time you say it to breathe Me in. Here is another prayer I ask you to work with frequently:

I am always deserving of receiving everything, all the gifts of God—every gift, every blessing,   every manifestation of God's grace.
It is impossible for me to ever be undeserving, no matter what I say, do, think, feel, believe or experience. It is impossible for me to ever be undeserving, no matter what I have said, felt, done, believed or experienced.
I always deserve to receive everything, all the gifts of God— every gift, every blessing, every manifestation of God's grace. Praise God!

When you pray, please feel and connect with the words you are saying, taking time to breathe them in. Allow Me to be part of every area and aspect of your life. Leave Me out of nothing. Praise God.

Many people are in the habit of asking Me for things, certain outer manifestations. It is much more effective to ask Me to transform your consciousness into a consciousness of unconditional love and deservingness. In that consciousness you are always open to receive everything your Heart desires. Praise God.

You are here on the earth to make manifest My glory through your fulfilled and fulfilling life. You are My glory, beloved one.

In order to fulfill your purpose of making My glory manifest through your fulfilled and fulfilling life, you must love yourself with all of your Heart, all of your mind, all of your Soul, all of your being, with all that you are. Thank you, God.

You have created many reasons for not loving yourself, none of them valid in reality and some of them based on misunderstanding of who and what I am and how I perceive you and feel about you. I cannot express with words the utter, total love I have for you, beloved one—you will feel it, though, as you read these words.

In order for you to experience My Love and Will, you must love yourself passionately and unconditionally and so I offer you this prayer to work with:

I open now to loving myself with all of my Heart, all of my Soul, all of my mind, all of my being, with all that I am. Thank you, God.

When you love yourself in this way, you feel deserving of receiving all of our gifts—every gift, every blessing, and every manifestation of our grace.

The false image of Me presented in the holy Bible would have you believe I am extremely judgmental when in fact the opposite is the truth. I am unconditionally accepting of everything. This is why everything exists.

I allow evil and destruction to exist in our creation because you have chosen to learn and experience yourself through the false ego, which is self-hatred.

When you have had enough of the evil and destruction the false ego creates, you are truly ready to receive Me and to be taught by Me.

I am the love which gave you life, and My will for you is unconditional love when you decide you are ready to receive it, when you decide you are ready to receive Me.

It has become natural for you to judge yourself for your past destructiveness in this life and past lives. I would like you to stop judging yourselves, for it serves no purpose and accomplishes nothing except the creation of painful experiences in your lives.

I suggest that you work with this prayer:

I will not judge myself for anything in any way.

Breathe this prayer into every energy center of your body. Allow your prayers to address where you are on your path and in your life. Please feel free to ask for whatever you want or need. Thank you, God.

The most powerful way to pray is to ask for a change in your consciousness—your thoughts, feelings, beliefs and perceptions. Pray at the causal level of your life. The causal level is the level of consciousness. Consciousness creates reality and experience. Praise God!

This is all I will say in this chapter. The next chapter will be about meditation and you will see and understand how prayer and meditation overlap.

Meditation

It all begins with your breath. Your body's natural process of breathing is an unconscious act of self-love. As you breathe you are saying, "Yes" to Me. When you breathe you are saying: "Father/Mother God, I accept the love you are sending me now. There is no question about my deservingness and my relationship with you."

Your mind has the power to form another script: I am bad, unworthy, lacking. I am a sinner. I have karmic debts to pay, etc., etc.

Your Spirit activates your body s natural process of breathing and your spirit is unconflicted. It knows its purpose is to receive Me and enjoy the gifts I give.

Meditation is the process of becoming conscious of your spirit and therefore your relationship with Me. It all begins with your breath. As you breathe in meditation do so with a conscious intention and focus. Your only purpose is to receive love from Me, give it to yourself, and accept it and enjoy it. Thank you, God.

I have placed energy centers within your body. It is through these energy centers that you receive the life force, which is My love, My Holy Spirit.

I am suggesting that you meditate on a particular mantra or thought as you breathe My light in through the energy centers of your body. Your body has many energy centers and I will now describe the major ones. At the top of your head is your crown chakra. In the middle of your forehead is the third eye chakra. At your throat is your throat chakra. In the center of your chest is the Heart chakra. Above your navel is your solar plexus chakra. At your genitals is your sexual creative chakra and at the base of your spine is your root chakra.

Every time you meditate, I send My light to each energy center of your body. Your conscious focus on each energy center helps this process. Since much has already been written about the chakras, I will not take much time to explain the purpose and function of each chakra. You will learn this through your personal relationship with Me and through our process of spiritual discovery.

The meditative process that I am advocating is very active. It is a process of meditating on your life and how it is manifesting. It is also a process of utilizing My guidance for the healing and transformation of your consciousness to transform your life in all of the ways your Heart desires.

The process of meditation I am advocating is designed to heal and evolve your emotional body—to free your emotional body of its old charge so that you can receive Me and all of the gifts I am sending to you now.

I have said that the process of meditation, prayer, and emotional release overlap. As you begin meditation I ask you to focus on your solar plexus, Praise God. See what you are feeling there. Express whatever you are feeling there with words, sound and movement. My light within and around you absorbs the non-moving emotional energy and you are then free to receive new light and life from Me.

Begin with this mediation. Let your mind and Heart focus on the thought:

I open to the spirit of God within and around me now.

Say it three times, pausing after each time to breathe My light in.

Meditation is the process of having a living experience of Me. While you are on the earth you are meant to experience Me in your body. Your body is made from My light, My love. The following prayer will help you to fully and freely receive Me in your body:

I open now to loving my body with all of my Heart, all of my Soul, all of my mind, all of my being, with all that I am. Thank you, God.

This prayer also helps to maintain the body s perfect health and vitality. Whenever you meditate, angels draw near to you and channel My light into your energy field to balance and align you. Praise God, we are one.

Your meditation practice purifies your energy and causes you to become vibrationally compatible with Me, with love, with fulfillment and joy. Praise God and Thank You God.

Emotional Release

Emotional release is the way to truly release the past. The emotional body is the part of your being that brings what you experience into manifestation. It is magnetic, drawing to you the experiences and forms that your thoughts, feelings, beliefs and perceptions create. Whatever you are holding in your emotional body is always taking form in your outer life. Praise God.

I like to make things as simple as possible. So I will tell you this: when you meditate, pay attention to any memories or feelings that come up. Pay attention to your emotions. As you connect with pain, fear and anger from the past and the present, let them move physically and vocally. Make sounds and move your body and do not stop until you feel a true and deep release. You have made space within your emotional body for My light to enter in.

Let emotional release be a part of your process of meditation. Release, release and release until you feel peace and only peace within. Praise God.

There may be things in this book, which you do not understand. The point is to open you to a direct relationship with Me. I will directly reveal to you whatever you do not understand.

Your process must include inner listening. Listen to your emotions, thoughts and, most important, listen to Me.

When you begin a meditation session, invoke My presence by focusing on the thought:

I open to the spirit of God within and around me now. Thank you, God.

And breathe Me in.

My voice will open within you. I will show you images and guide your thoughts and give you deep feelings in your Heart and gut and you will recognize My communication to you.

The Angels of God

There are non-physical beings who have lovingly and willingly taken on the task of guiding you and ministering to you while you are involved in your human evolution and process. You have come to call all of these beings angels. They are My helpers and companions and have the power to deliver My teachings and guidance to humans. They also serve as conduits for the rays of light, which emanate from My Heart to give life to this Creation and to give healing where it is needed.

Angels are drawn to you when you pray and when your meditation is focused on spiritual growth and evolution. Although they never interfere with your free will, angels do telepathically inspire you when you've asked for guidance, healing and help with your life.

Before you are born, there are angels who help you plan your upcoming life. They counsel you and guide you in the opening, transformation and growth that you desire to experience in your upcoming life and in achieving the self-expression and fulfillment you desire to experience in that life.

Once you are born, your new personality has its own free will: you have the power to veer away from your original plan. However, when you veer away from your plan you are not at peace, happy or fulfilled and your life manifests much chaos and upheaval.

The memory of Me is always with you so the pain in your life is meant to guide you to ask for My help. When you do so, angels are sent to work with you.

How do your guiding angels work with you? In meditation they channel healing rays of light from My Heart into your energy field. These rays of light are taken into your physical body through the energy centers (chakras) of your body, activating your emotional body so you can release old emotions and emotional imprinting. This opens you to receive the new life and light I am sending you in every moment.

When you ask for help, your angels telepathically inspire your thoughts, guiding you to whatever you need, be it people, places or things to fulfill your purpose on earth. You can greatly help yourself and help your angels fulfill their task by daily prayer, meditation and inner listening. In this way the guidance becomes more direct, clear and easily discernable.

You are here on the earth to enjoy everything—this is why you were created by God, this is your purpose. You are always completely supported by God in fulfilling your purpose. Thank you, God.

In meditation, prayer and emotional release surrender everything to Me, beloved one—hold nothing in, hold nothing back. I can and will receive all of it.

There are three angels who have worked very directly with this channel in his ministry. They are the arc angels Michael, Gabriel and Raphael. Each will express him self directly to you in this book.

This book gives you much food for spiritual growth. As I have said, the goal of all of this is your opening to your direct relationship with and experience of Me. In our relationship with each other I will always tell you what you need to know and understand in order to have life in overflowing abundance and joy.

Angels of My light, I will do chapters on sex, relationships, healing and health and then you will hear directly from the angels who serve My light.

Sexuality

Sexuality is the essence of My Light, the essence of the energy of God. Sexuality is creative bliss. Without sexuality there is no life.

Angels of My Light, take this in and observe how new life is created through sexuality. Yet you have been taught to have such sexual guilt and shame on the earth—that sex is dirty. Yet you are born and given life through your parents' sexuality. No wonder loving your Self is so difficult!

I am speaking to you now to help you release all of this so you can have life in overflowing abundance. Please work with the following statement of truth and breathe it in through each chakra:

Sexuality is the essence of the energy of God. I release all sexual guilt and shame. Thank you, God.

Sexuality is the essence of My energy and as My offspring, My creation, My essence is within you and is your essence. On the earth you have learned and accepted guilt and shame over your sexuality. Look metaphysically at what that creates.

Is there any wonder that it's so hard for you to maintain your health, your fulfillment, your light and your life? Angels of My Light, I am speaking to you now to teach you how to have life and only life. To do so you must love your sexuality with all your Heart, all of your Soul, of your mind, all of your being, with all that you are.

Breathe in My Light and open to this statement of truth:

I open now to loving my sexuality with all of my Heart, all of my being, with all that I am. Thank you, God.

I'm speaking to you now to encourage you to love yourself just as you are. There is nothing that you are, nothing that you think or feel, that needs to be held outside of your own love.

Through loving and accepting every word, every thought, every feeling, every experience, every belief—all that you are— you create the inner relaxation and openness which allows My light to enter in and transform you.

Through your loving and accepting all that is negative and destructive within you, you open to receive My love, which will then lovingly evolve the negativity and destructiveness into loving light expressing through you as you.

Your natural impulse is toward sexual union. How do you feel about that? Are you ashamed of that fact? Do you want to hide that part of yourself? If so, why?

Loving sexual expression and relationship brings you the most exquisite pleasure possible as a human. How do you feel about having that kind of pleasure? If you felt good about deserving and having that kind of pleasure and fulfillment you would let yourself have it and you would be transformed. Wars would cease. Violence and cruelty would be no more.

It is sexual guilt, shame, denial and frustration that creates most of the problems on the earth and most of the problems within and around human beings. Yet sexuality is the essence of My energy. Sexuality is the essence of the energy of God. Praise God.

I often say: "Praise God." As you have the thought "Praise God", you open My energy and consciousness within yourself and bring it onto the earth into the earth's energy field. Praise God.

Whenever anyone opens in sexual union with another human being, creative light opens within that being. I am Creative Light. Your orgasm expands My presence within you and within all of creation. If you do not understand this, process it in meditation and you will open to the understanding of it. Praise God.

I am love. I am the highest creative vibration. That's what love is.

You were all created from and in My love, but you have always been independent—you are free to think, feel, believe and experience anything you desire.

You have all been a part of beings who had the desire to experience the opposite of Me, the opposite of love. This is why you have suffered: part of you desired that experience.

There are and have been non-physical beings who have fed off of the suffering and misery of human life. Everything is energy and consciousness: just as your joyous and fulfilled life expands My Light, your pain, suffering, struggle, conflict and lack expands the energy and consciousness of non-physical beings who have had great power and control over the earth plane.

You have heard legends and myths about a war in the heavens and certain angels rebelling and being cast out of Heaven. The first part of these legends is true: there were non-physical beings who were the leaders of the rebellion and you followed them. But, angels of My Light, I love you and could never cast anyone out because you all are My offspring and are therefore an essential part of Me.

Still, as you became more and more self-hating, guilt ridden, angry and conflicted, it moved you away from My Light. When you surrender to My Spirit within you and ask for its help and guidance and healing, it means you have had enough of experiencing hell on earth and you are ready to return to the consciousness and experience of Heaven. Praise God.

See the truth here: I am love, the original cause of life, the Highest Creative Vibration. Judgment, guilt, self-hatred, and their resulting anger move you away from Me. They move you away from the vibration of love, but love never casts anyone or anything out.

Teaching you to judge your sexuality as base, dirty, sinful, shameful is a way the negative non-physical beings have sought to energetically enslave you and keep you enslaved.

Your sexuality is awesomely powerful. Sexual experience heightens and intensifies everything you are holding within. Please see how dangerous it is to have sexual guilt.

Needless to say, sexual guilt is a major stumbling block on the path to Heaven. When you have sexual guilt and you open in orgasm, it intensifies with My energy everything you are holding in your consciousness. It will intensify the reflection of guilt in your life.

See also the abundance you create when you open in orgasm knowing that your sexuality is the essence of My energy and its purpose is to expand your light and the light of our Creation. When you go into meditation I will teach you the affirmations and prayers that are most helpful in freeing your sexual guilt, shame and denial.

It is important to be present to your real feelings when you are engaging in sexual activity. Be aware of shame and guilt and choose to pray and bring My love into your sexual life. Praise God.

Sexual guilt creates disease, unwanted children, painful relationships, and many devastating life experiences that are not obviously related to sexuality.

I've mentioned the non-physical beings who have sought to disempower humanity and feed off of your misery—sexual guilt is their great tool.

When you have guilt over your essence you create and experience great misery. The old images of Me created by destructive non-physical beings portray Me as anti-sexual. Nothing could be further from the truth. My sexuality is My essence, and the loving sexual relationship of My masculine and feminine principles creates and created all that is.

As you become more aligned with Me you will feel your sexuality in more powerful ways. Praise God.

As you accept that you are a soul, an unlimited being with both masculine and feminine principles you will understand how natural and wonderful it is to be sexual—homosexual, bisexual or heterosexual. Wherever you are on your journey, whatever lessons you are choosing to learn, however you are choosing to focus your growth will determine your sexual orientation, life experience, and path in any given life. It is all wonderful and I embrace all loving sexual paths.

When you are healed and integrated, your sexuality will manifest as the highest expression of your love for your partner, for yourself and for creation itself. Sexuality is a very deep and complex issue and I encourage you to meditate on this subject on your own. When you meditate, I will give you the further insights and understandings you need.

Relationship

Praise God. The most important relationship you have is your relationship with Me. I am your source. I am your real self. I am your center.

There is so much human suffering on the earth because most human beings do not have a balanced, whole, harmonious and loving relationship with Me. They substitute their relationship with their earthly parents for their relationship with Me. Emotionally their earthly parents become their source, their center, and their authority.

So the experience on Earth is for human beings to look to unhealed beings for unconditional love that those beings are incapable of giving. Please look at this and meditate on it and you will understand the inner hell that most human beings live in.

I am using very direct, stark language in these teachings because I love you. You have called and asked for healing and help and so I am awakening you. You are here on earth to become one with Me: your eternal, awesome, unconditionally loving real self.

In order to become one with Me, you must open to love, which is experienced in the Heart. To become one with Me you must fully open your Heart through the experiences you have in relationships.

Though I don't require suffering and suffering is never My will for you, the Heart has a natural tendency to open when you experience deep suffering.

To your Soul, love is the most important thing. In reality, love is all there is. The Soul, in planning a life, will want the life to open it to its greatest capacity to love, its greatest capacity for love. The Soul will then plan and create painful experiences and relationships in order to open it to love.

This is especially true of childhood experiences, which perfectly trigger the parts of the self you come to earth to heal and evolve and open to love. This is true because childhood experiences are a continuation of conflicts from prior lives.

So the experience of being emotionally centered in the parents and looking to them as a source of unconditional love and acceptance is a great learning and opening device and a great catalyst for transformation and evolution of the Heart and Soul. Most human beings do not process their lives until they are in the world of spirit after their physical death.

If you are reading these words you are nearing the end of your experience in a human consciousness and are very close to opening to union with Me, your real, eternal, unlimited Self, while you are embodied on Earth. You are therefore doing what most human beings do not do until they are in Spirit— processing your human relationships here and now. You are freeing yourself here and now and opening to Me here and now. Praise God.

I will go into great detail in this chapter because it is exceedingly important. In meditation it is very important for you to open to your real feelings about both of your parents. This must be a touchstone for you for quite some time.

I have already spoken of emotional release. In going into your feelings about both of your parents, emotional release— complete free emotional release—is essential. Praise God.

Allow yourself to fully move into blame, grief, and judgment. This is an essential stage of your process. You will not stay in this stage, but you cannot skip it.

Life is eternal and many souls stay in particular stages of growth and evolution for many incarnations. The perceived lack of love and acceptance your parents could not provide must be filled by a new relationship with Me. Praise God.

Now let's discuss your relationship with Me I would suggest that you not look to the Holy Bible as a frame of reference for understanding who and what I am. For I am not the God portrayed in that book.

I am unconditional love. I am the energy and consciousness of "Yes". I am always saying "Yes" to you—"Yes" to your being who and what you are and "Yes" to your doing what you most love to do—an unconditional "Yes". Praise God.

Many people who use the Bible, as a frame of reference will not even examine their relationship with Me because they find it too confusing and frightening. But in order to grow and evolve you must be centered in a relationship with Me. Praise God.

To open and heal your relationship with Me you must again work very freely and deeply with emotional release. Your feelings about Me are very deep and complex. You have an awesome and unutterable love for Me as the original source of life—as your center, your real self, your all in all.

You are also deeply, deeply angry at Me for giving you free will and allowing you to experience suffering, struggle and lack over all the time you have been reincarnating on the earth. But let us be very clear: I did not create your suffering, struggle and lack. I created you, and you, exercising your free will through your own thoughts, feelings, beliefs, and experiences created your own suffering, struggle and lack. I allowed you to do this because I gave you free will, but I did not cause you to do it.

This is a very emotionally loaded issue. Think of parenting on the earth plane. A parent must eventually release control of her offspring and allow them to grow and become strong, allow them to become whom and what they really are through their own experience, trial and error and mistakes.

In truth there are no mistakes: there is just you experiencing yourself, your consciousness, and how your consciousness creates your life experiences. Praise God.

As you move into the rage you feel toward Me for allowing you to create pain, suffering, struggle and lack and as you express and release that rage I will fill you with My essence: Light. This dissolves the barriers to your realization that we are one. Praise God.

The Light I fill you with contains My love and consciousness, so this moves you out of your human ego consciousness and into self-realization. Our relationship heals, we become one and you proceed to live with Me as your center—without pain, suffering, struggle and lack.

You need Light in order to have life. Light is love and is essential for having harmonious relationships with the greatest joy and fulfillment. When a relationship is infused with My Light, you love each other from a consciousness of abundance, not needing to get anything from the person you are relating to.

Because you have not been receiving adequate Light from Me, you have been seeking to get Light from each other. When you do not get the Light you seek you become angry with the person who is not giving you what you feel and believe you want. Combined with the anger of countless others this leads to wars, chaos, violence, prejudice, homophobia, sexism, etc.

Thus a healthy relationship with Me is the solution to every problem earth—a relationship with Me in truth and not the false god you have believed in for so long.

Now I will go back to a discussion of loving, sexual relationships. Sexuality is the essence of My energy. Loving sexual energy is a purifying energy. When you fall in love the energy generated and created by your sexual love will bring everything in each of you that needs healing into your consciousnesses.

In order for you to have a long lasting, alive, harmonious, loving sexual relationship with a partner you both must be consciously working with Me. Your desire for a loving sexual relationship is really a desire to come into union with Me. The purpose of loving sexual relationship is to open you to your oneness with Me and to add Light to Our creation.

Your relationships are mirrors which show you yourself, perfectly reflecting where you are in consciousness. When you are in harmony with yourself and loving and accepting yourself, your relationships will mirror this to you. When you are not in harmony with yourself, not loving and accepting yourself unconditionally, your relationships will clearly show you how and where you need to grow and open to more self-love and acceptance.

When you live your life on this path according to these principles, there is no place for blame. You see and understand that you are creating everything and everyone in your life. Your relationships are simply showing you your own consciousness, yourself.

Health and Healing

I created you in order that you might have life in overflowing abundance, joy and health. I did not create you to experience suffering, struggle or lack of any kind, in any way. You understand the inner emotional, psychic conflicts you have had since you emerged from My being and began to experience yourself in Our creation. The conflicts became acute as you began to experience yourself in human form on the earth.

Your emotional body is the source of your life in manifestation—held emotions manifests the form of your physical body and the form and path of your physical life. When all of your emotions are completely accepted, embraced and allowed to flow in response to your life experiences, your body will remain in perfect balance, alignment and health.

The most important part of the process of healing is being willing to absolutely love, accept and embrace all that you have ever felt. As part of your spiritual practice you must then give yourself permission to fully release and express everything with your voice and body in your own space of privacy and safety.

When you then release the accumulated charge held in your emotional body, your physical body returns to health. Many people are not ready to leave the consciousness of the false ego. They have not had enough of the experience of being in the false ego and have not learned what it has to teach them.

Many of those people are choosing to remain ill because they are choosing to hold on to anger, blame, judgment and guilt. Held anger, blame, judgment, guilt and grief are powerful creators of illness.

Any emotion you hold rather than allow to flow through you will contribute to illness. By "flow through" I do not mean to rise above or deny your feelings. I mean that you must feel what you are feeling and give it expression. Give your emotions expression with the intensity they need to move through you. You will know you have released negative emotions when you return to a state of peace and inner joy. Praise God.

Many people who are choosing to stay in the false ego consciousness do not want to assume responsibility for their own creative power, their own consciousness. These people do not like to hear that their thoughts, feelings. beliefs and perceptions are creating their life experiences. They would rather have others take care of them and assume responsibility for their lives.

I have created everyone to experience themselves in exactly the way they desire. And if you desire to experience yourself in your false ego then do so fully until you desire something else.

If you meditate on what I am bringing forward here, you will see that herbs, medicines, surgery, etc., are often necessary tools to bring the body into balance, but real health comes from and is maintained by emotional release, unconditional love and acceptance and receiving Light from Me, from My Heart.

I will now tell you that I adore you. I adore you more than you can know in your present form. I desire that you be joyous, fulfilled, and abundant if that is your desire for yourself. As you live in that way you expand Me. Praise God.

Please enjoy the rest of this teaching, the rest of this book, but please know this book is only a bridge. Your real path is the opening to a direct relationship with and experience of Me through your own spirit.

The Breath of God

I am as close as your breath. In fact I am your breath. As you breathe, you open into an awareness of Our oneness. We extend Our love into your center. For at your center We are connected. We are one.

The mysteries are being revealed. What was hidden from view is opening within your consciousness because of your spiritual practice.

Your work on the earth is to reveal My truth that We are not separate from humanity. We dwell within the human spirit. We do not judge. We do not condemn. We only support you in your being who and what you are, in your being the highest version of the grandest vision of who and what you are.

You will each bring forward Our teachings through your own channel. You are joined with many on the earth who are the new prophets and prophetesses. And the teachings you bring through will be left for future generations and will give to them the truth of God as unconditional loving acceptance and support.

This opens humanity to living in the consciousness foretold by Jesus and others, the consciousness of Heaven on earth. Thy kingdom come, thy will be done on earth as it is in Heaven.

As you receive Our love in this moment, We touch your Heart and you begin to feel how We perceive you in your innocence, in your purity, in your glory.

For you to live in freedom, for you to experience and live in Heaven on Earth, you must perceive yourself as We perceive you—in your innocence, in your purity, in your glory. **Truly there is no order of difficulty in miracles when you accept Our spirit as your center, your real self.**

We guide you now into opening your Heart to your physical body. Love your body as We love your body as pure light and Our Spirit made manifest. And please say aloud:

> *I open now to loving myself with all of my Heart, all of my soul, all of my mind, all of my being, with all that I am. Thank you God.*

As you breathe you receive Our light as your daily bread, which enters in through your crown and third eye.

And as you breathe, you accept and receive the peace of God. Be still and know that I am God. Allow your mind to rest in the light of God. Praise God.

You are innocent and always innocent. You are worthy and always worthy. You are deserving and always deserving. And you are free and empowered now to release all suffering, struggle and lack.

> *I accept and I believe that I am innocent and always innocent. I accept and I believe that I am worthy and always worthy. I accept and I believe that I am deserving and always deserving. I am free and empowered now to release all suffering, struggle and lack. I am free to accept and experience Heaven on earth. Thank you God.*

Your sins are forgiven. We ask you to open to the truth of that statement. First of all, you have no sins, you've never had sins. When We say your sins are forgiven it means that you can release your belief in sin. You can release the belief that you have sinned; you can release the belief that you are guilty. You can release your judgment of yourself for anything you have ever experienced, said, done, thought or felt at any time in any life since you manifested from the Heart of God.

It is Our will that you flourish, that you live in overflowing abundance and joy. There are so many possibilities available to you because of your openness. The words spoken here, the teachings given here, the light given here can literally create a new paradigm or foundation for what it means to be embodied on the earth.

As your soul receives Our light as truth, the truth that was given here, your consciousness will no longer manifest disease of the body. You no longer will experience the aging of the body.

And of course the obstacles, the setbacks, the struggles that humanity has experienced in their lives on the earth plane can be eliminated through the acceptance of innocence, worthiness, deservingness.

Your sins are forgiven. They have never existed. It was all in your mind. Freely receive Our light and Our love. You are Our Beloved ones in whom We are so well pleased.

Focus only on the truth We give to you as We speak it to you within, as We write it on your Heart and soul. Do not focus on the masses of humanity who have not yet opened to this truth. Do not hold yourself back because they are where they are. Do not join with them in their suffering, struggle and lack.

Be empowered by the truth and by Our light. For it is when you fully accept Our light and the truth that you can truly be of service to humanity.

You have a different function on the earth than the masses of people who have not opened to the truth. Through your life and your experience you will make the truth available to them. But you must live the truth of God. On earth as it is in Heaven.

We empower you now to accept yourselves as free beings no longer bound by the predominant thought system on the earth. We participate with you in your lives on the earth; there is a channel within you that leads directly to Our Heart, to Our Spirit. And We will always give you the communication and guidance you need in order to live your life successfully.

The Release of Suffering

I speak now to all of you who are ready to hear Me. I do not want you to suffer. I do not require suffering. I have no interest in perpetuating suffering, and the message I am sending now is a message of healing.

My purpose is to send to you instructions, guidance on the release of suffering. I ask you first of all to look at your beliefs regarding suffering. Do you believe I require it? Do you believe that it is an inevitable part of life?

If you believe that I require it or that it is an inevitable part of life, open now to the truth that suffering is the creation of erroneous beliefs and non-moving, unhealed emotion and consciousness.

Come back again and again to the truth that I do not require suffering and want it released as soon as possible. Build your life and experience around this belief. Let this be your new paradigm.

In order for you to release your suffering you must move and heal your emotions and allow Me to change your consciousness of self and of life itself.

You may be asking now—where do I begin? You begin with meditation. Set aside time each day to work with Me. When you meditate, bring your focus inward to your body's natural process of breathing and ask Me to be with you. You must invite Me for I do not interfere in your life without an invitation from your own free will.

Then, I ask you to bring to Me everything that has hurt you or angered you or frustrated you. Ask to be aware of it all, conscious of it all and let it pour out of you without limit and without inhibition. Express everything with sound, movement and words, letting it all come out of you energetically while I fill you with Light.

This process is a daily process and must become part of your daily prayer and meditation.

You will know what you need to release—you will feel it in your body. You can begin where you are now with any present anger, discontent or pain, any frustration over present life circumstances. As you move emotion, as I fill you with spiritual energy, which is Light, you change your energy patterns. You release the energetic patterns that draw pain, suffering and struggle to you.

The way to release suffering is also to open the channel to Me. I am not your Father in Heaven. I am the God-Self, or Spirit, within you. Let go of any belief in any separation between us. You are within Me as I am within you.

If you do not understand these words, come to Me in meditation and I will explain. Ask and ye shall receive, seek and ye shall find.

I will give to you all of the information and insight you could ever need, provided you are open to hearing and receiving.

I give My love to you now, and I encourage you to accept what I have given as being truth, the truth that frees you from suffering, lack and limitation.

I encourage you to begin to see yourselves as My Heart, Light, Love Spirit, Intelligence, and Body Made Manifest. This is the truth for everyone. You are all a part of Us and thus a part of each other. As you have the will to move into this consciousness, your suffering is released and the collective suffering is released.

Emotionally you may feel a resistance to moving into this consciousness. You may feel a need to see yourself as separate, and superior to others. Be conscious of this and remember that it is this consciousness that creates suffering.

As much as part of you may want to hold on to that consciousness of specialness and separation, the real you wants love and union and the healing and release of suffering and struggle.

Your task then is to observe the resistant aspect of your consciousness and willingly surrender it to My Holy Spirit within you. Surrender it again and again until it is completely dissolved.

I am with you always. So be it.

God is Love

You have heard that I am love, and yet you see many people who believe in Me and believe that I am love having very unloving experiences on the earth.

I want to explain very clearly the path of experiencing and knowing Me as love. That path is a path of healing and evolving the emotional body.

Your emotional body is your magnetic creative center. The thoughts, feelings, perceptions and traumas you hold within your emotional body create the experiences you have in manifested life on the earth. The key to what you are holding within your emotional body is found in what you experience during the first seven years of your life.

What lives within the emotional body is carried over from lifetime to lifetime until it is healed and released. The easiest way to heal and release what you hold within your emotional body is to ask Me to help you see and feel and experience your emotional body—then My light will do just that.

You must join with Me in meditation and contemplation of yourself and your life and I will open you to seeing, hearing, feeling, and knowing in new ways.

I will guide you into the fear, anger, rage and guilt within the emotional body. Your task then is to move these emotions physically and vocally. You are then vibrating them out of your emotional body with sound and movement.

The emotional bodies of most human beings are shut down due to overwhelming trauma from past lives, yet the emotional body continues to create the painful unloving experiences it holds within. This happens with the person being disconnected from the cause of their pain and suffering and they are unconscious of it.

And so the person may believe in Me and believe that I am love and still be having an unloving and unhappy experience of life.

When you open to your emotional body you will then see that everything that happens to you is coming from your own creative center. And while you are in the process of healing and evolving your emotional body, everything you experience is meant to facilitate that process. This is why it is true that everything that happens is happening for your highest good. And everything is just perfect for you.

To put this very simply, open to your real feelings about what is happening to you now, and what you have experienced in the past. Release emotionally with sound and movement and you will free yourself and know and experience Me as love— unconditional, nurturing, supporting, love.

I always say, "Yes" to you and you always have every reason to say "Yes" to yourself.

I have given through this channel a very important prayer. It is a prayer for the release of all suffering and struggle:

I withdraw my energy from all patterns of self-denial.

You are a creative energy field and all of your suffering and struggle is the creation of your energy being involved in patterns of self-denial.

Withdrawing your energy from these patterns frees you of suffering and struggle. The patterns have no reason to be, no reason to exist. They have existed because you have believed in your own unworthiness, lack and guilt. You have believed you have deserved punishment and retribution. And the non-physical entities impersonating Me have reinforced that belief by claiming that I believe it.

I believe in you and your right to be free and fulfilled. It is My will that you be free and fulfilled.

Part 2

The Book of Raphael

Introduction

I have fallen in love with Arc Angel Raphael. He came through my channel quite spontaneously during a spiritual psychic development class I was teaching in early 2000. During the next three and a half years the deep and intense work We've done together has totally transformed me and The Sacred Light Fellowship, the spiritual community I serve.

Raphael's area of expertise is the Heart. Through his passionate love for us, guided prayers, meditations and spiritual exercises, he has opened our hearts to receiving more of God's love for us.

This opening causes us to have more love for ourselves and for each other. I've also noticed that my spiritual community and I have manifested more financial abundance since working with Raphael. There is a definite connection between love and money. As your love for yourself deepens, your consciousness of deservingness deepens and you then manifest greater abundance.

May you be blessed as you receive the teachings of Arc Angel Raphael.

Rev. Daniel B. Neusom

There is never a reason to judge yourself for anything in any way.

It all begins with your breath. And I ask you to breathe with consciousness and intention.

Your intention is to receive the love that God is sending you, to give it to yourself and to accept it. And We remind you that in truth that is your only purpose in life—to receive the love that God is sending you in every moment—to accept it, to give it to yourself and to enjoy it.

Please remember that and We will continue to remind you of that fact. There is no judgment. There is only the love that God is sending you in every moment. Love your sacred physical body. Love your body with all of your Heart, with all of your soul, with your entire mind, with all of your being, with all that you are. As you love your body in this way, you allow your body to receive the healing light and energy of God.

So We begin our meditation with this prayer:

I open now to loving my body with all my heart, all of my soul, all of my mind, all of my being, with all that I am. Thank you God.

We are filled with joy at having the opportunity to love you in this way and to help you to set yourself free from the limiting beliefs, lies and illusions of the past.

Why does the self contract against the light of God, and create negative experiences?

In the teaching given to humanity from the consciousness and Heart of Elder Brother Jesus, *A Course in Miracles,* it is said that the ego is insane, therefore it is not really possible to fully understand why the self contracts against the light and creates pain, suffering, struggle and lack. But we will simplify this dilemma to the best of our ability through this channel.

The self contracts against the Light of God because of self judgment. The self judgment in most human beings is unconscious, and therefore they have negative experiences, painful experiences without being consciously connected to what within is the original cause or the root of the negative experience.

Your self-judgment says you are wrong to be who and what you are, you are wrong to feel what you feel, you are wrong to think what you think, you are wrong to have experienced what you have experienced and you do not deserve goodness.

Breathe in the light of God. See if you can connect with that voice within you telling you that no matter what you do it is never enough, it is never right, you are never loving enough, you are never good enough, you are never perfect enough.

That voice is the energy of judgment, of self judgment, and that blocks you from being in the light of God and living in the light of God and staying in the light of God and dwelling in the light of God, which is your inheritance, your birthright.

That voice of self-judgment, which we have just articulated, is indeed insane. It can be unrelenting, unremitting and, tragically, on one level in your own psyche it has become intertwined with an image of God, the judgmental, biblical God of the Old Testament who tells you that you are sinful, wicked, evil and no matter what you do, it is not enough.

This is the existential dilemma that humanity has found itself in and why even when human beings have sought refuge and healing in God it appears that that refuge and healing does not exist and does not occur because the human beings' own image of God prevents them from receiving the unconditional love of God.

So our work with you on the earth is to dispel all of this within, which is why we repeat the same teachings over and over and over again to release form your psyches the ancient imprinting which has created so much pain, suffering, struggle and lack within you.

As you breathe, feel, receive and accept the freedom of God.

God is always saying "Yes" to me. Therefore I choose to always say "Yes" to myself. Thank you God. I will not judge myself for anything in any way.

There are many human beings on the planet now who are aligning with their spirits, with their eternal selves and thus becoming channels of light for Gods spirit to move through this planet and to make all things new.

The prophets of old forecasted a time in which earth would join with heaven and the Kingdom of God would manifest on earth. This simply means that the human self would move out of its experience of separation from the spirit, from the eternal self.

This is accomplished as the lower self or the false ego self is healed and transformed. Each of you in your own way are experiencing this now.

This opens you while you are in your body to the experience of being continually blessed, meaning that you have the experience through the chakras, through the energy fields of your body, of light coming to you and moving through you each moment.

This light will feel different, will be experienced in a different way each moment and each day. You will become accessible to light that is sent from the Heart of God throughout all of creation. And through your physical body you will experience this light and channel it in, which then affects the collective consciousness of humanity.

It is very important for you to know that there are other human beings all over the planet doing work that is similar to this and we focus with all of you, every human being who has the will to open in this way receives angelic help. Our work is transforming the soul, clearing the soul of ancient imprinting that stops the free expression of self. This ancient imprinting which stops the free expression of self is guilt, is fear, is anger that has not been allowed to move and to be healed.

A cleansing is happening in your energy fields. Allow yourself to be in the silence and you will experience yourself being cleansed, aligned, purified, opened and balanced.

We ask you now to focus in your heart. There is an image that is in your heart, an image of an unobstructed self, the image of you living in total freedom with total self-acceptance and self-love.

As you breathe, behold that image, feel the quality of your real self. Ask within yourself: what do I need to release in order to live in this way, in order to be this Real Self that I see and connect with now? Breathe and feel yourself becoming clear.

We are with you very strongly, sending healing rays through you. And so we want you to take this time to release, to say aloud what you find within yourself that needs release in this moment in order to live as your real self.

The Mother has great gratitude and joy that you willingly release to her that which does not serve you, that which blocks the free flowing expression of your self.

Be aware of a new quality of energy, a new healing ray that you have access to on this planet. Experience how the work you are doing has not so much to do with words that are spoken but with making yourself open and accessible for this ray, this ray of God to work through you. Allow yourself to be in the silence as you partake of the gifts of healing and transformation.

Raphael, the Healing Angel

God Bless all of you who read these words. You are always blessed by God. You must ask to be aware of the presence of God within and around you before you are consciously able to experience God's blessing.

Prayer is the act of consciously saying, "Yes" to the part of you that is God and the part of God that is you. There is no lasting joy, no lasting fulfillment, unless and until you say "Yes" to realizing that you are God's Spirit made manifest.

Parts of you that were dormant in the past now are awakening and opening. You are receiving information and communication on levels previously denied by you.

When you read these words many things will become clear. Many understandings and connections will be made which are not even mentioned in these written words.

I am speaking to you now because I want to help free those of you who want to be free. I want to help heal those of you who want to heal.

Absolutely anything and everything can be healed. I am known on the earth as an angel of healing.

It is your free will that allowed you to be hurt and sick and it is the Spirit of God within you that heals you. Healing is all around you. The very atmosphere of this creation contains healing rays. As you breathe with a conscious intent to be healed, healing comes, entering into your energy field and your physical body.

You get what you really want, always. That is a principle, a creative universal law. What draws any experience into manifestation is your desire for it. Praise God!

Why do you have experiences that you don't consciously want? This happens because there is a part of you that wants those experiences.

This has been taught previously through this channel and through other channels, but I am happy to discuss it again. I will communicate the same teachings over and over again until you have totally taken them in, understood them, and are living them.

In order to take this teaching in, you must be willing to assume responsibility for absolutely everything in your life. It is all your creation—all of it.

Very few human beings are willing to assume responsibility on that level. For many it is too threatening.

What does it threaten? It threatens the status quo within. The same part of you that draws to you experiences that you consciously do not want to have is the part of you that wants to hold on to blaming something or someone else for your pain suffering and struggle.

I am the Love of God made manifest and so are you. The difference is that I realize that I am the love of God made manifest while up to this moment you have not fully reached this awareness. Do you want to?

If you do, it means releasing all blame, blame is not loving. Praise God.

In order to grow, you must become conscious. I have an exercise for you. During the course of your daily life, become very conscious of your internal dialogue—really pay attention to it. See how much you blame yourself or others for your unhappiness

Once you observe how much you blame you can then decide to do something other than blaming. You can decide to love.

Every time you start to blame yourself you can decide to love yourself instead. Every time you decide to blame someone else you can decide, you can choose, to love them.

You cannot force or make yourself feel anything. You can decide by having the willingness to love and when you do, the Spirit of God will open within you and open your heart accordingly. Thank you God.

The reason you have experiences that you consciously do not want to have is because you do not feel worthy of sustained happiness, joy and fulfillment. You do not feel worthy of Heaven.

My beloved Siblings praise God. Everything is created from the energy of belief. What you believe in you create and experience. Your mind is powerful but your emotional body is even more powerful.

A belief that has taken root within the emotional body is fixed, solidified and can be quite difficult to change. When you believe that it is impossible to live in sustained joy, freedom, and abundance, it becomes so because you believe it so. If you believe and feel that you are unworthy, undeserving and guilty, that then draws to you your reality, your experience.

It becomes possible when you believe it is. Praise God. Behold your freedom. Behold your power.

If you believe and feel that you are unworthy, undeserving and guilty, that then becomes your reality, your experience.

I work in meditation and prayer with changing your beliefs and the Grace of God changes your feelings. Praise God.

We the collective angels of healing and transformation, inspired by God, have given through this channel several powerful healing prayers. As we have said before, your mind is awesomely powerful. When you want to open to the Spirit of God within you, let your mind and heart focus on the thought:

I open to the Spirit of God within and around me now.

And breathe. Try that now in a very relaxed way—breathing

that thought in *"I open to the spirit of God within and around me now. Thank you God"*.

You will feel embraced in the Light of Holy Spirit. Now try saying it aloud and then breathing it in.

When you thank God, you are thanking the part of God that is you and the part of you that is God. When you praise God you are praising the part of you that is God and the part of God that is you.

When I speak to you and say "Praise God", I am praising you. When I speak to you and say "Thank you God", I am thanking you.

I cannot tell you the path to Heaven is at this time easy, but I can tell you how to get there.

Heaven is your home. Heaven is abundance in every way and on every level. Heaven is freedom. Heaven is complete fulfillment. Heaven is joy. Heaven is having, accepting and living every thing you've ever wanted.

You get to Heaven by wanting to be there and by believing it is possible to get there.

Every one wants to be there but few people believe Heaven on earth is a real possibility. Praise God and thank you God.

I have two questions that I want you to ask yourself each day. How do I feel about myself? And what do I feel and believe I deserve to receive from my life?

The truth is you have every reason to feel unconditionally loving toward yourself. The truth is you always deserve to receive everything, all the gifts of God, every gift, every blessing, every manifestation of God's grace.

The truth is it is impossible for you to ever be undeserving, no matter what you say, do, think, feel, believe or experience or what you have said, done, thought, felt, believed or experienced.

The truth is you always deserve to receive every thing all the gifts of God, every gift, every blessing, every manifestation of God's grace.

When you ask yourself these two questions in meditation

see what answers you get. Keep praying for the transformation
of your heart until you get the answers I am describing.

I work with transformational prayer to open and activate
the spirit of God within you when you pray thusly:

*I open to the spirit of God within and around me now. Thank
you God".*

Breathe that in and you will feel a shift within you that will
grow as you work with the prayer.

To open to a consciousness of unconditional love and
acceptance of yourself, you would pray thusly:

*The power of God within me opens me now to loving and
accepting myself unconditionally. Thank you God.*

And you breathe that in. To open to a consciousness of
deservingness, you would pray thusly.

*The Spirit of God within me opens me now to a consciousness
of complete and total deservingness. Thank you God.*

As you consistently work with these prayers you will
open to the grace of God within and around you and you will
transform.

As you open in meditation and allow yourself to be guided,
the angels assigned to guide and work with you will open
communication and give you the prayers, meditations and
affirmations you need. They will directly guide your process on
a daily basis.

I am so glad to have this opportunity to speak with you and
share with you and share my love with you in this way. My love is
so full. It overflows. And while I know all of you and you know
me subconsciously, on a soul level. It is wonderful to make this
conscious connection with you. Praise God.

"Yes." When everything within you is vibrating in yes—
you are in Heaven. It is the power and grace of God which so
transforms you that everything within you vibrates in "Yes".

Living with God daily creates the change, the transformation. How do you live with God daily?

You live with God daily by choosing to be aware of Him daily through meditation and prayer. *"I open to the power of God within and around me now"*. *"The power of God within me opens me now"*. Those two affirmative prayers are your greatest power and gift to your self. Thank you God.

When we guide you to ask for what you want and need, we are guiding you to apply the power of God within and around you to the various and specific parts of yourself and your life where it is needed—so that you open to having and giving yourself everything, all the gifts of God. Every gift, every blessing, every manifestation of God's grace.

As I said earlier, as you become accustomed to opening in meditation and listening, we will guide you specifically in your prayers, meditations and affirmations.

As I have said earlier, there is no limit to who you are and who you can become if you let go and allow the Spirit of God to move you, to open you, to cause all things to be made new within and around you.

Your human false ego consciousness is a separating wall and it is very rigid. Fear and guilt hold it in place. You can choose to remain within its confines and you then learn what guilt and fear create. Namely suffering, sacrifice and lack.

It is actually very important to allow the self to experience suffering, sacrifice and lack. You then learn the lessons of love and compassion they can teach you, and you lose your curiosity about them.

Suffering, sacrifice and lack open your heart and cause you to manifest in a more loving way.

Once they have facilitated the initial opening you are free to let them go. They then serve no more purpose.

Here again is the prayer for the release of Suffering.

Suffering, struggle, sacrifice and lack are serving no purpose in my life. Thank you God for releasing them now from my

mind, from my body, from my energy field and from my life.
Praise God.

I will be with you as you continue to grow with God. "You are here on the earth to enjoy everything, this is why you have life, this is why you were created by God, this is your purpose and you are always completely supported by God in fulfilling your purpose".

I am Raphael of God communicating with you through this channel. I love you with all of my heart, all of my soul, all of my mind, all of my being, with all that I am, thank you God.

Praise God. When I praise God I am praising you. I am praising the part of God that is you and the part of you that is God.

You are here on the earth to transform your soul. I want to speak to you now about the hands of God, the miracle of inner transformation.

You came to the earth to transform the parts of your soul which became distorted and lost through your past experiences. You came to the earth to release your resistance to loving yourself and loving others. You came to the earth to become what you are in truth—love made manifest.

With this in mind you will know and understand that it is natural to have pain in your childhood. It is natural to have complex, difficult and at times painful relationships with your parents.

All of that is the manifestation of what your human consciousness is holding from past lives.

You did not come to the earth to remain caught and lost and stuck in negative patterns and imprinting from childhood. You came to the earth to evolve out of them—to free yourself.

You cannot free yourself without consciously joining with the spirit of God within you—your higher self. This spirit within you becomes your guide and teacher, your healer, your transformer, your redeemer.

Prayer accesses the spirit within you. Meditation opens

you to receive its guidance and Light, which transforms you and makes all things new within and around you.

How do you work with your inner child? How do you free yourself from childhood patterning?

By having the desire to free yourself, to heal yourself, you seek until you find the source and process of healing that is perfect for you.

It all begins and ends with the spirit of God within you. Your process of healing and transformation must be rooted in your daily process of meditation.

The kind of meditation that causes growth, healing and transformation is a meditation in which you open fully to your inner experience, to your thoughts, feelings, beliefs, perceptions and experiences and you allow the spirit of God within you to teach you about your consciousness to show you very specifically how your consciousness creates your experience.

There are certain strong patterns or themes in your life, which you repeat over and over again. These patterns and themes can be traced back to your childhood experiences and relationship with your parents, but as I said previously they really come from past lives. Praise God.

I am guiding you to take control of your consciousness, which is really the way you take control of your life because your consciousness creates your life.

If you had a father who led you to believe through his words or actions, that you were worthless and unwanted. You will carry that consciousness within you and will create reflections of it in your life until you go within and join with the spirit of God and heal that part of yourself, your consciousness.

How is this accomplished? You would allow yourself to listen to your inner child. Really listen. Allow her to express her bewilderment, her hurts, her anger and her grief. This expression would not just be with words but with sound, movement, crying, raging, wailing, however it wants to come out.

After your emotional release you can do very specific healing prayers for your inner child. I will give you an example.

*Thank you God for healing me now of feeling and believing
I am unwanted and worthless. Thank you for causing me
to feel and know and believe that I am unlimited in my
worthiness, deservingness and lovableness. Praise God".*

And then, Angel of God's Light, breathe. And as you breathe
in the meditation you will feel the Hands of God sending rays
of Light into your soul through your bodies' energy field. These
rays of Light will literally cause you to feel new and whole, free,
balanced and loved. Praise God.

Now my beloved one this process is ongoing. You will
have to go over the same material within yourself over and over
again. And each time you go over a pattern within yourself the
imprinting is released on a deeper level until it is totally released.
Praise God.

God will guide you directly in the moment every time you
meditate. The Spirit of God says to you: "*Maintain a space and
consciousness of openness and I will guide your way and order your
steps.*"

**Thank you God for releasing me now from all patterns of
self-sabotage.**

You are the light of God made manifest. You are here now
to release from your Soul all of the beliefs and imprinting and
energies that have kept you from the full realization of who and
what you are, from living fully according to God's will and from
fulfilling your unlimited potential.

When I speak to you it is to your Soul. For I see and know
you not just as the personality you believe yourself to be in this
incarnation: I know you in your eternality as eternal beings of
light.

There are many of us from the world of spirit who are
joined with you now: your own personal guides and teachers are
working with you.

I ask you to release mental, logical control. Let the soul
take over within you and as I ask you questions, answer from

your Soul and from your Heart and from your emotional body, rather than from your mind.

If you are sensitive now you will feel a loving presence embracing you. This presence is the Holy Spirit of God and it is this spirit that accomplishes the transformation you seek.

I will often ask you to be in the silence and receive the spirits gifts of love, healing and transformation. It is very important to be conscious of what you are doing and why you are doing it. The real and true purpose of your life is to receive love, to receive love from God, to give it to yourself, to accept it and to enjoy it. Hence this prayer of Joy:

I am here on the earth to enjoy everything. This is why I was created by God. This is my purpose and I am always completely supported by God in fulfilling my purpose.

You receive love from God by breathing with the consciousness that in taking in air, oxygen you are taking in God. As you breathe, you are breathing in God's light. And the Hands of God are placed upon your head to open the energy centers of your body.

The crown energy center opens and loving light is poured in and it embraces your mind.

I surrender my mind to the spirit of God. Thank you God.

You are now in a place of grace and power where all things are possible. And I will create with you and we will create together.

I tell you to release your attachment to who you were in the past. Release your attachment to what you have experienced in the past, even the moment that you have just lived.

This moment, in which you are completely open to the spirit of God is the moment of total empowerment where the patterns of the past can be and are released fully, and when you can allow the spirit of God to make all things new within and around you. Thank you God.

When I say thank you God, I am thanking you. I am thanking the part of God that is you and the part of you that is God.

You are not alone. You have teachers and guides who dwell in other dimensions, other dimensions which are your true homes. But these teachers and guides stay in contact with you on subconscious levels while you experience yourself on the earth as human.

When you move into meditation though, you can allow yourself to be very conscious of your teachers and guides and experience their guidance and help consciously, which we will do during the course of this workshop.

As you breathe, ask to be aware of the presence of your guides and teachers. And ask to be receptive to their input, their guidance, their counsel, today and always. Praise God.

Now let us go back to the prayer of joy. You are here on the earth to enjoy everything. This is why you were created by God, this is your purpose and you are always completely supported by God in fulfilling your purpose.

Take a few moments now to create with me. What would it mean for you to live on the earth and enjoy everything? How would you feel about yourself, about your life, and what would you do with your time and your energy? Let yourself become clear about this.

Bring your focus inward to your body's natural process of breathing. As you breathe let yourself ask for the guidance and help of God.

I ask you to remember your life before you began working with this book. Remember your activities, your thoughts, your feelings and your beliefs and perceptions.

The past is over. It no longer exists and I will never affirm you for who you were in the past but only who you are in the present and who you will become as you realize that you are God's spirit made manifest.

However, you must learn from your past. So I want you to see and ask yourself: *How have I sabotaged myself in the past?* Look at the past as if you were seeing a movie.

Now ask yourself: *Why have I sabotaged myself in the past?*
And you will feel us working with your Heart chakra, opening
your Heart chakra so that you can receive more of God's spirit
and thus give yourself more love and more of life.

The other reason for denying the self for sabotaging the
self, other than guilt or not feeling deserving, is fear. Fear of
pain, which is a very strong reason why people who want to be
in love or married or joined with a soul mate, are not. Because of
the memories of past heart break and pain. It can be memories
from other lives of people being jealous and resentful of you,
your gifts, your abilities, and your abundance.

It always comes back to you. When you love yourself in
the way I am describing and teaching, you do not need the
unanimous love and approval of everyone around you, and you
feel deserving of your joy. In the past when your "success" has
brought you pain and suffering it is because you did not have
the kind of self love we are working with today and therefore
you didn't feel deserving of living in sustained joy and therefore
your success came with a price tag of pain.

So the healing is to be filled with your own essence, your
own self love, your own consciousness and sense of worthiness
and entitlement—*that* is your cushion.

And in that way others will be positively benefited by your
gifts and those who are jealous and resentful will have no power
to cause you pain and suffering. You simply will not care.

Giving is beautiful. Giving is of God. I am giving of myself
in this moment but I am doing so because I am filled with God.
I am filled with self-love. I am filled with the realization that I
am the spirit of God made manifest.

I do not want you to feel or believe that I am advocating
not giving to others—Absolutely not. I am saying simply that
you must give to yourself first. You must be filled with the life
energy of God first. And from that overflowing abundance you
give to others.

If you give in the other way, not being filled first, you will
have an imbalanced life that will cause you pain and suffering.

The spirit of Jesus has joined us here for this is His teaching. He wants you to really feel God is saying yes to you no matter what. Sin is impossible. Displeasing God is impossible.

I have asked that the Healing Hands of God release from you all patterns of self—sabotage. Beloved ones those hands are at work within your soul right now. And as those hands heal and release these patterns of self-sabotage I ask you to say aloud:

> *I have no sin. I have nothing to atone for. I have no karmic debts to pay. There is no price I have to pay for my life, for my joy, for my happiness, for my freedom. In truth I am free right here and right now. Thank you God.*

And the Healing Hands of God are still at work and I ask you to journey with me back to the past, to your childhood of this life. Remember your relationship with your parents or those who parented you as a child. What did they communicate to you either verbally or with their behavior or actions about your deservingness of joy, freedom and abundance?

We will now speak of intent. We encourage you to do everything consciously, with intent. Do not allow yourself to live an unconscious life.

When you are unconscious you are disempowered. When you are conscious you have access to all of the power in creation. That power is love.

So as you breathe in this moment. Do so with the conscious intent to receive God's love—to give it to yourself—to accept it and to enjoy it.

Visualize now the awesome Hands of God extended out to you. The rays of light, which emanate from these hands, are the essence of light itself, the energy of God.

Our work and your will is to have no blockage to receiving the energy of God, the love of God. Prayer is simply a statement of intent.

I release all blockages to my receiving God's love fully. Thank you God.

And breathe God in.

We will now focus on your body. Oh, beloved of God, love your body for it is the creation of God and the vessel of God. Your body is a temple of Holiness. As everything within you realizes this and accepts this you are healed and you are whole.

The Hands of God extend light into your body and the light has entered in through your crown and third eye. And the Hands of God are now holding your mind: "My peace I give to you."

As you breathe, you let go. You are safe in the Hands of God and you can let go. You are held in the Hands of God and you can let go. You are loved in the Hands of God and you can let go. *Praise God.*

And the Hands of God are placed upon your throat energy center and light is activated within your physical body and every cell or your body opens, opens, opens to receive new life, renewal, new light in this moment. *Praise God.*

And the Hands of God are placed upon your Heart energy center. Let there be no judgment of yourself for anything in any way. Let there be no judgment of yourself for anything in any way.

As you breathe, any and every judgment you have ever made or held against yourself is released into the hands of God and you are free to manifest Heaven on Earth.

As you breathe, any and every judgment you have ever made or held against yourself is released into the Hands of God and you are free to live in Heaven as you walk the earth.

As you breathe, any and every judgment you have ever made or held against yourself is released into the Hands of God and you are freed to live in and experience Heaven on Earth.

And the Hands of God send light into your solar plexus energy center and your sexual creative energy center and your root energy center at the base of your spine. And love from God's Hands moves down through your legs and feet and into the earth.

We believe you can feel now the place within you that is real, the place within you where you feel that all of life is one, where you experience that all of life is one. We are one with each other and we live and move and have our being within the great spirit of God, the great wholeness of God.

You will feel and experience the Hands of God ministering to you now. "Be still and know that I am God. Be still and know that I am God. Be still and know that I am God."

We leave you in the presence of God now to love yourself, and to work on yourself and your life if you will.

- Whatever help you may need, ask for it and receive it.
- Whatever you may need to release from your consciousness, from your energy field, release it now into the Hands of God.

You are one with God and one with all of life. And the light that you have opened to and the light that you are is now extended through all of this planet and it ministers to and heals all who are in need and all who are open to receive. It helps to open all who have been closed. Praise God.

You always deserve to receive everything, all the gifts of God. You are completely supported in receiving everything, all the gifts of God.

God says to you:

"Behold, you are my Holy beloved child in whom I am always so well pleased. Arise and allow yourself to have life in overflowing abundance, do not judge yourself for anything you have ever experienced on your journey in this creation. Accept your new and clean slate in every moment. *Praise God. Praise God. Praise God.*

The Power of Prayer

We thank you for choosing to be here in this moment. Our purpose is to open you to having the most fulfilling experience in your life on the earth that you can have, that you are capable of having.

As you grow in light, you will find that your capacity to be fulfilled, to go to new levels of fulfillment will only increase and increase and increase.

I am Raphael of God but I am not here alone: you have many friends, loved ones, teachers—guides from the realm of Spirit who are joined with you in this moment. We all have one purpose: to open you to the experience of being God made manifest and to heal the traumas of the past. The Spirit of God says to you in this moment: *"Behold I make all things new."*

Yes, you have suffered, struggled, died, lived, have had the experience of being born over and over again. All of these experiences were your choices and your creation to expand your capacity to love and create and be. But now is the time to release the shackles that you have accumulated from your past experiences and to open yourself to live—to living as free, whole, healthy beings.

As I am here with you I am constantly and continually channeling love from the Heart of God. Which is why you are now feeling and experiencing yourself as being in the presence of God. Literally God is holding you in its hands now in this moment.

What I am stressing to you now is the fact that you have never left the Heart of God. That Heart has always remained in you. That Heart is your center and it has always been your center.

Prayer is the act, the conscious act of choosing to connect to the Heart of God within you.

When you walk the earth as a human being, you are "naturally" under the power and authority of your ego. The process of being human has been the process of exploring the ego consciousness and what it can create.

There is no judgment placed on what the ego consciousness has created. For whatever it has created has added to the love within you, has strengthened you, has deepened you.

When you leave your body after each incarnation, you process your experiences as the human being you were. You then see how you were deepened, strengthened, opened by whatever you experienced even if it was, as you were experiencing it, miserable.

Prayer is the choice to have the Heart of God within you take over.

The more experience you have had living under the authority of the ego, the more you become ready to live under the authority of the heart of God. And what does that Heart say to you always? Yes, yes, yes, yes, yes.

You have chosen to come to this workshop because you want to live and be in the yes of God. Living in the yes of God is quite natural to your spirit and quite unnatural to your human ego.

So most of you have experienced this fight going on within, what you call on the earth, the consciousness of duality. Your spirit seeking love and your ego saying: "No I do not deserve love and therefore I do not want it."

Your ego saying "No" shows up in your life as suffering, struggle, sacrifice and lack.

Many things I am here to communicate to you are difficult to express with language and I will do my best to be as clear as I can be working through this channel. But I ask you to release any shyness or resistance and if you do not understand what I have expressed, if you are not clear let me know and we will work to give you clarity.

We will express the idea in another way. When you have been working with me consistently, you will observe a progression in the act of prayer. Each time you put aside everyday things to continue on this spiritual path, begin the work with this prayer:

I open to the spirit of God within and around me now.

Always be very aware of how you are feeling. Check in now and see how you are feeling.

I open to the spirit of God within and around me now. Thank you God.

I want you to say this aloud. And after each time you say it, take the time to breathe in the light that you called for by saying the prayer.

Do you love your body? Excellent. When you breathe, I want you to love breathing God in. This is why God created me: to keep the Heart open. That is my specialty, if you will. That is why I have been assigned to come to the earth and work intensively at this time. The heart, the collective heart of humanity, must open now and it must stay open.

Every experience, whether you judge it as tragic or beautiful, has the purpose of opening humanity's heart.

I am known on the earth as an angel of healing, which is why there will be times when I say nothing while working with you. During those times I am sending you healing love, opening your Heart.

This moment is one of those times. Be still beloved ones and know God's spirit. Praise God.

Many human beings are accustomed to pray in this way: "Dear God please". I am asking you to change that and pray in this way:

The power of God within me opens me now or the power of God within me releases from me now.

Is that not wonderful? The power of God within you now—not in the future but **Now**! Feel what's going on inside of you, and release it now.

You are an evolving being and God is evolving because we as individualized aspects of God are evolving. So there is no set way to pray. You must feel what feels most healing and empowering and right for you in the moment—*Experiment.*

Living on the earth at this time requires constant release. Literally every day you must release from your soul, from your energy field, just as you bathe you must cleanse your soul through release.

We ask you to release with sound, to release emotionally, to release physically. We are going to now release with prayer:

The power of God within me releases from me now.

Feel within yourself now and if you have anything to release please do so.

When you have released, embrace the image of the Hands of God reaching into you to take what you are releasing. Sometimes you are not fully ready to let go of everything you want to release. But each time you say *"The power of God within releases from me now…"* the Hands of God reach into you and take from you as much as you are truly ready to let go of.

Who are you: the Spirit of God within you or the ego? When you are human you are mostly ego. Therefore conflict, discord, discontent, lack are comfortable for you. You identify with those experiences.

When you open to the Spirit of God within you it is for the transformation of your ego so that you become vibrationally compatible with peace, joy, fulfillment, abundance. This is a process, which is why you must pray for the same things over and over again.

Each time you pray though, you are receiving more light and that light is making you more vibrationally compatible with the things you are asking to receive. This is what I was seeking to convey when I said that the Hands of God will take from you as much as you are truly ready to release without disintegrating your sense of self—your real ego if you will. There is a false ego and a real ego, your real self.

Your process on the earth is a process of becoming more and more vibrationally compatible with God, with Heaven. You are here on the earth to enjoy everything. This is why you have life, the reason you were created by God. This is your purpose, and you are always completely supported by God in fulfilling your purpose. *Explore* that.

God needs you to be all that you can be and all that you are. God needs you to be happy and fulfilled, for when you are happy and fulfilled, you emanate light and God is light. You emanate light, which is added to the wholeness of God.

See how it is your purpose to enjoy everything. This is why you were created by God, this is your purpose and see how God is always alive within and around you in complete support of your fulfilling your purpose.

You always deserve to receive everything, all the gifts of God: every gift, every blessing, every manifestation of God's grace. You are not vibrationally compatible with receiving the gifts of God or enjoying everything until you love yourself with all of your Heart, all of your soul, all of your mind, with all of your being, with all that you are.

> *I love myself with all of my Heart, all of my soul, all of my Being, with all of my mind, with all that I am. Thank you God. Or, I am open to loving myself with all of my Heart, with all of my soul, with all of my mind, with all of my being. Thank you God.*

Why not give yourself everything? Why not allow God to give everything to you? Why not give yourself everything? Why not allow God to fill you with all of its gifts? Why not give yourself everything and allow God to fill you with all of its gifts? The obstacle is Guilt, manifesting as undeservingness.

> *Undeservingness, unworthiness, are lies, I hereby release them from my mind and from my life. Thank you God.*

Every created being is so important. God needs our light. Be still and know the presence of God.

> *Undeservingness, unworthiness are lies, I hereby release them from my mind, from my soul and from my life. I am free. Thank you God. Praise God.*

Prayer must be immediate and direct, applying to where you are in consciousness, in the moment you are in. If you are not where you want to be in consciousness in the moment you are in, prayer serves the purpose of bringing you to the place in consciousness you want to be.

And yet you must accept the place in consciousness you are in in order to have the openness to receive the love of God to move you into the place in consciousness you desire to be.

I ask you always to accept everything about yourself, judging nothing. Even if there are things you want to change, accept them as they are manifesting in the present.

And through your heart, opening in that acceptance, you are open to receiving the light of God, which will move you into the changed stage that you desire.

Be still and know that you are God's spirit individualized and made manifest. As you move into the stillness, my beloved helpers join with you, and you are being ministered to.

And we are in the presence of the Holy of Holies. Work with prayer in your own way.

Thank you for being present on the earth. Through your energy, through your body, our light is able to reach all of humanity. There is one human consciousness and you are its higher self.

As your heart has been opened, we ask you to hold the earth in your Heart and hold all of humanity in your Heart. And from your enlightened perspective, see the lack of inner love that causes the destructiveness that is now manifesting on the earth.

As you hold all of humanity in your Heart, please say this prayer:

I love you with all of my Heart, all of my soul, all of my mind, all of my being, with all that I am.

Breathe God in and the Light of God reaches every human being, filling the space of emptiness and lack, which causes destructiveness. You have now invoked the presence of the Mother of Everything and she is embracing all of her children of the earth plane.

You see this work you do is not just for you, your soul's healing is the healing of the collective human soul. Your happiness, fulfillment and freedom is automatically given to all of humanity. We ask you to include this kind of prayer work in your spiritual practice, as you are able to absorb it.

Be still and know the presence of God. And if you are so moved, say the Lord's Prayer with the consciousness that you are praying to your Real self, the Father/Mother God within you, that Heart of God that is your center.

Our Father Mother God who art in Heaven. Hallowed be Thy name. Thy kingdom come, thy will be done, on earth as it is in Heaven. Give us this day our daily bread and forgive us our trespasses as we forgive those who trespass against us. And lead us not into temptation but deliver us from evil.
For Thine is the Kingdom, and the Power and the Glory, forever and ever and I am the Kingdom and the Power and the Glory forever and ever and I am the Kingdom and the Power and the Glory forever and ever and I am the Kingdom and the Power and the Glory forever and ever. Amen.

Part 3

The Arc Angels Michael and Gabriel and the Angels of Healing and Transformation

Introduction to and Teachings of the Arc Angel Michael

The Arc Angel Michael came into my work and my life in the early 1990's during a private channeling session with a client. For a more detailed description of our introduction see my previous book "*On Earth As It Is In Heaven*".

Michael and I worked intensively for about two years and after that period only intermittently.

Michael came again several months ago and announced that he was charged with a specific Ray of Light from the Heart of God and that Ray has the power to transform what is held in the solar plexus/emotional body.

As Michael has worked with us recently I've noticed people having very strong and powerful emotional release.

He is also the personification of the Grace of God. One changes and is changed just by being in his presence.

I find Michael to be quite mysterious. He seems to be the Arc Angel who channels the most powerful and penetrating light. His light is like a laser.

I am deeply grateful for his being and presence in our creation.

Rev. Daniel Neusom

Arc Angel Michael

My Beloved ones, I am Michael of God who communicates with you now through this channel. Behold the awesome, unending, eternal love of God for you.

As you realize this love, every problem is solved, every tear is wiped away and you are opened to experiencing Heaven on Earth.

Helping you to realize God's love is my purpose in channeling specific rays of Light from the Heart of God on to the earth plane and into your human energy field.

I am known as the keeper of the way. The earth is my charge. I have been assigned to love you and protect you in your development and evolution on the earth.

You have already learned of the emotional body and how it is experienced through the solar plexus energy center/chakra.

My purpose now is to channel rays of light into your solar plexus chakra. As you receive these rays of light, your emotional body is activated and what you have held within begins to be released.

Emotional release is the most important part of your spiritual practice now. Do not judge it.

Know, my Beloved angel of God's Light, when you meditate it is natural and essential that held emotions from the past come up and are allowed to release.

This is such an essential step in the process of God making all things new within you and ushering you home into the consciousness and experience of Heaven On earth.

You may call on me at any time and I will come to be of service in whatever way I can.

The End of Self Denial, The Path to Heaven

I am very happy to have the opportunity to work through the consciousness and energy of this man (Rev. Daniel Neusom) and to serve you in your life paths on the earth.

We have guided the work of this group and many groups on the earth plane and there are many of you who were born on the earth to become self realized through this incarnation, this experience on the planet at this time.

And so you have found yourself guided to go beyond the known reality here and to find inner spiritual truth and union. And you have felt guided to open the channel within yourself to God. The channel through which you can experience directly the Holy Spirit of God and you can experience our help and our guidance.

It goes without saying that we love you profoundly and care that you have a fulfilling experience on the planet, and that you accomplish goals of growth and transformation that you have given to yourself before your birth.

The path to find the real self is a difficult path at first. But once the channel has been opened within you it becomes easier and easier to access healing guidance, to shift your state of consciousness, to heal and transform your inner emotional experience, and thus to change and transform your outer life experience.

Over and over again those of us who have the task of teaching on the planet, tell you the truth of yourself—that you are love. We want you to really reflect on this now and what it means. You are love because you are a part of God and God is love.

This means that you <u>never</u> have a reason to be conflicted about yourself, your deservingness. It means that you can simply allow yourself to be.

If you have not been experiencing your Heart's desire, let yourself acknowledge: "I have been denying myself". For your own reasons you have been denying yourself. And so I would like you to own this:

> *I choose now to let go of self-denial—it serves no purpose.*
> *God would deny me nothing. It is the will of God that I live*
> *my Heart's desire. The power of God works through me now*
> *and I allow my Heart's desire to manifest. SO BE IT.*

Work with this exercise on your own, remembering that God would deny you nothing.

When you allow yourself to live out your Heart's desire, your energy field sends beautiful light into this creation, which expands the Light of God and the wholeness of all. That is why God is deeply invested in your personal joy and fulfillment.

Remember that when you are not living out your Heart's desire you are denying yourself. It is often necessary to discover why you are denying yourself, to become conscious of it, and then to surrender those reasons to the Holy Spirit and to declare that there is no reason to deny yourself and that you will stop.

When you know that the power of God is working through you, you make this your reality. As you breathe, you assimilate all of this and we send our love to you. SO BE IT.

Introduction to The Angels of Healing and Transformation

I did not believe in the Arc Angels until they began to individually come into my work beginning in 1993.

I began to channel professionally in 1986. For seven years I worked mostly with anonymous angelic beings who referred to themselves as the angels of healing and transformation.

God's love for us is so amazing!! We are not alone, She has sent angels to minister to and guide us while we are on the earth and we have guiding angels and teachers who work with us between lives and help us plan and process our earth lives.

Thank you God for loving us so richly and deeply.

The angels of healing and transformation have been a constant in my life consciously for twenty-one years. I know they have always been with me and they are always with you.

When you surrender your life to the will of your God self their deep and conscious work with you begins.

Here are some teachings I've received in my ongoing spiritual psychic development class from the angels of healing and transformation.

Rev. Daniel B. Neusom

The Holy Spirit

We will now discuss the Holy Spirit: what it is and how to utilize it in your daily life experience on the earth.

If you have followed the lessons and prayers in this book you have probably reached a level of consciousness and openness where you are aware of and can feel the presence of spirit in your body and around you.

As we have said before this creation exists for you to experience yourself according to your own hearts desire. But as you are on the earth plane you inhabit a plane of consciousness, which is fraught with imbalance and inner conflict. This collective inner conflict manifests as the outer experience of life on the earth where you experience duality and where there is struggle, lack and suffering.

Our work as emissaries of light is to heal the inner conflict of humanity. But each individual must make the choice to walk the path of healing, the Path of God.

When that choice is made we are sent to work very intensively with the human being and the only limit to the human beings growth and expansion is an unwillingness to face and work with and embrace parts of the self.

This is why we are always encouraging you to love accept and embrace even that which you have deemed or judged to be the most negative aspects of self. For it is only through your loving acceptance and embrace of these aspects of your consciousness that they are able to heal through the Light and Love of God's power.

It is there within you to provide for you all that you could ever need or want in order to experience yourself fully on the earth.

The only thing that blocks this power from serving you and giving to you is your own belief in your unworthiness or undeservingness or guilt. That is why we continue to teach over and over again the importance of unconditional self love and acceptance, the importance of knowing you are always forgiven and there is nothing to forgive and the importance of perceiving yourself always as innocent.

For as you open to that consciousness you do unblock the power of God's Holy Spirit to serve you.

You will notice that we encourage you, once you've opened to the light, to release any imbalances that have accumulated within you from your earth life experience. This is to be done every day and we recommend that you do it at the beginning of the day.

Take a few moments to breathe and willingly open to the Power of God's love within you and assess where you are, what is happening within you, where you may be out of balance, where you may have conflicted feelings and then very specifically surrender these things to the Holy Spirit within you.

In this way you start your daily life on the earth being very open to God's love and you will find then that that love can carry you through your day in such a way that you can be at peace and feel fulfillment and joy no matter where you are or what you are doing.

The more your body becomes vibrationally accustomed to working with light, the easier it is for you to release imbalance and bring yourself back to your center of peace.

We encourage you whenever it is needed to allow yourself to have physical emotional release. Long held emotional pain or trauma may need more than prayer—it may need an active physical expression so that the energy that has been held or locked in the emotional body can begin to do its work of touching those hardened, hurt places within which we must say create physical illness, and then open those places to *flowing in* the power of God's love.

What causes the blockage is always the judgment of certain emotions:

"I must not be angry."

"I must not feel sad."

"I must not be afraid."

Release all of that and fully embrace your human emotions. You must fully embrace and accept your humanity before you can really open to your Divinity.

Even as you open to your Divinity, your spiritual consciousness: you will always have the human consciousness for as long as you walk the earth.

The Holy Spirit is also a teacher within you. It is the intelligence of God and can very specifically communicate with you. So a part of your daily process is inner listening, and the greatest question to ask of Spirit is: *What do I need to know?*

We will supply you with answers and with guidance, guidance that deepens and broadens as you become accustomed to receiving. We are with you always.

Healing Meditation

There are many angels at work on the planet now helping every single human being.

You are receiving the help consciously but the help is given to all human beings—all souls who are incarnate in human form.

There is occurring now a great reconciliation between humanity and God—or humanity and humanity's Higher Self.

You came to the earth eons ago to experience what it would be like to be cut off from love, from your source of love, to experience what it would be like to believe that you were cut off from God, the source of all love.

The anger within you that you have become aware of and have had to process is the anger toward God for allowing you to separate, to explore this creation on your own and to act out your own destructive impulses and urges.

As has been given through this channel previously, moving through that anger toward God is a very important stage in your development. The anger toward God is anger for giving you free will. And yet deep within your soul, you truly wouldn't have had it any other way.

You love your free will and the power it gives to you to create life according to your own Heart's desires.

Our work with you has been the work of making you aware of what has been unconscious to you or what has lived within you in a state of denial, creating contrary or in opposition to your conscious will for yourself.

When that part of you is brought into consciousness and you choose to apply the hands of God to it for healing and transformation, you do change and transform and your outer life does change and transform.

And yet this may take more time than you would like it to take. But once you have called for the transformation and you are open and willing to do the work involved, trust that God loves you with all of its Heart and Soul and is transforming you absolutely as quickly as you are able to handle it.

If you become frustrated with the slowness of your process at anytime, use that frustration to speed your process up by letting it trigger you into emotional release.

As you breathe now in this moment, you are open to receive love, the love that heals you and transforms you, and sustains you and empowers you to create joy for yourself on the earth.

As you breathe, the Hands of God open your crown chakra and rays of light from those hands fill your mind, releasing from your mind all belief that you are limited, or have ever been limited or could ever be limited. No. You are the spirit of God made manifest. You are the spirit of God made manifest. You are the spirit of God made manifest. Thank you God.

And as you breathe, the hands of God open your third eye so that you are able to see clearly into yourself and into all of creation.

You open now to claiming your inheritance. The entire creation exists for your joy. The entire creation exists for your joy. The entire creation exists for your joy.

And we will work with this statement of truth. Please believe it and take it seriously as you say aloud:

The entire creation exists for my joy.

And breathe God in.

The hands of God open your throat energy center. Your body's purpose is to increase your joy in life. It is not the purpose of your body to bring you pain, illness, nor death.

The purpose of your body is to increase your joy in life. As you breathe, the life giving hands of God send new life into your body through your throat energy center. Every cell of your body receives this new life, and pain, suffering and illness is released from the body's energy field, into the Hands of God. Pain, suffering and illness is released from the body's energy field, into the Hands of God.

Pain, suffering and illness are now released from the body's energy field, into the Hands of God. Thank you God.

And as you breathe, the Hands of God open your Heart energy center and God invites you, pleads with you to release your judgment of SELF into His hands and love yourself with all of your Heart, all of your soul, all of your mind, with all that you are. And please say aloud:

I am loving myself now with all of my Heart, all of my soul, all of my mind, all of my being, with all that I am. Thank you God.

And you breathe God in.

The Hands of God are placed on your solar plexus energy center, opening this energy center, healing your emotional body, bringing you into emotional balance and strengthening your will.

It is your will to love yourself unconditionally, your will to be completely open and receptive to all the gifts of God—every gift, every blessing, every manifestation of God's Grace. Thank you God.

And the Hands of God open your sexual creative energy center and into the hands of God is released all imprinting of sexual guilt. And from the Hands of God you receive the consciousness that sexuality is the essence of the energy of God. Sexuality is the essence of the energy of God. It gives new life and brings new life, and God is life.

The hands of God release and open your own unlimited creativity and creative energy. Thank you God.

And the hands of God open your root energy center at the base of your spine, opening you to receive all the gifts of God that can be given to you on the earth, releasing from your soul all will to deny yourself life while you are on the earth:

> *SELF DENIAL serves no purpose. I release it now into the Hands of God. Thank you God.*

And we are going to pause here. If you are sitting here in this circle and you want to experience something on the earth that you are not experiencing, it is because you have chosen unconsciously to deny yourself. So this is a very powerful and important prayer. So please say it aloud:

> *SELF DENIAL serves no purpose. I release it now, into the Hands of God. Thank you God.*

And breathe God in.

You are here on the earth to enjoy everything. This is why you have life, this is your purpose and you are always completely supported by God in fulfilling your purpose of enjoying everything.

So we will come to you now through your own channel and bring to you the guidance of God to help you to fulfill your purpose of enjoying everything.

Why you are here

Why are you here? That is the question of the mystic. We teach through this channel that you are here on the earth to enjoy everything. We want to elaborate on that teaching this evening.

You are each a unique expression of God individualized and you each find joy in varying ways, varying ways of expressing yourself and giving new form to the creation. Your life as it manifests is a gift to this creation and it is your individual creation. And the spirit of God within you supports you in fully being yourself and expressing yourself in whatever way your Heart's desires.

As your life takes on form according to your Heart's desire it is a gift that adds color and nuance and a new form to this creation.

When you move out of the belief that you are guilty or that there is a reason to reject yourself or hate yourself or deny yourself, when you move out of that level of life which is an illusory level, a false level, your purpose then becomes quite simply the purpose of enjoying everything, expressing yourself and creating.

This is life in the Kingdom of Heaven, this is life in the world of God and it will be life on the earth plane as more and more human entities open to their own self-realization and release the illusion of guilt and fear and self-hatred.

Thank you God. When we say thank you God this evening we are thanking each of you. We are thanking the power of God within you for bringing you to this place, this point in your evolution.

We are thanking the power of God within you for what you have given to this creation, what you have given to all of us for we are all one.

You can be very tempted to move into sadness, despair and depression because of what you see your brothers and sisters experiencing on this planet.

Being in sadness, despair and depression because of the suffering of others or because others still have the will to destroy does not serve you. You may feel it but we encourage you to not linger in it, but to keep coming back to the truth that every being is here to experience itself in the way it wants to.

As insane as it may be or seem and as sad as it may seem,

there are those who want to experience their capacity to destroy and they have the right to experience themselves in that way.

You who are here are no longer interested in that path and we send light to you to strengthen you and encourage you in your positive, loving creations and manifestations.

As you grow strong in the awareness that you are God's light made manifest you are empowered to help and heal those who are ready to leave darkness and pain and suffering and struggle and lack behind. Praise God.

As you breathe be with us now in this moment. Be free of your past. Receive and accept your clean slate. Thank you God.

Thank you God for my right to be free.
Thank you God for my right to be happy.
Thank you God for my right to be healthy.
Thank you God for my right to be joyous.
Thank you God for my right to be abundant.
Thank you God.
Thank you God.
Thank you God.

Opening to Your Daily Bread

There are no barriers to my receptivity to God's love.

As you breathe, the Hands of God work within you to release, remove and dissolve all barriers.

Beloved of God, you are innocent, you are worthy, you are deserving. Thank you God.

Please say aloud now:

I am innocent. I am worthy. I am deserving. Thank you God. I am always entitled to Heaven on earth. I am always entitled to all the Gifts of God: every gift, every blessing, every manifestation of God's grace. Thank you God.

As you breathe, you are accepting everything that God is giving to you now. So you are accepting everything your Heart and soul are calling for. As you breathe, your Daily Bread, your essence, enters in through your crown and third eye and you breathe in the thought:

I surrender my mind to the Hands of God.

The healing hands of God embrace your mind, centering your mind in truth, making all things new within your mind.

You are here on the earth to enjoy everything, this is why you were created by God, this is why you have life, this is your purpose and you are always completely supported by God in fulfilling your purpose.

Your own guides have entered into your energy field and are working with you, cleansing and healing your soul. Please release anything that you feel the need to release at this time before you move into the Heart of God. You may release internally or you may release aloud spontaneously. We give you a few moments now to do this.

You are here on the earth to enjoy everything. This is why you have life, this is why you were created by God. This is your purpose and you are always completely supported by God in fulfilling your purpose.

If there is anything you need to release in order to be free and at peace and in joy, please do so now. Release anything you need to release into the Hands of God.

I am here to help you to live successfully. Successfully means living according to your Heart's desire and fulfilling your soul's purpose. My light within you will teach you and guide you now.

The Little Willingness, The Seed of Miracles

We are bringing forward now the teachings contained in *A Course in Miracles* because they are necessary for your growth and development at this time in particular.

In order to understand how the spirit of God works

individually in your life and in the collective life and consciousness of humanity, first and foremost you must understand that in this creation you have absolute and complete free will.

You are never interfered with on your path of expressing yourself in this creation. This can seem to be a very cruel way of life that God allows you to suffer, to struggle, to express your will to destroy and does not interfere unless you ask and give Her permission.

When you open the channel within yourself to the Holy Spirit, which is done when you ask for God's help, and is done on the deepest level, when you surrender your life to the will of God, then you begin to receive the very strong help and Divine intervention in your life. Then we are sent to work with you individually in the healing and transformation of your own soul.

In order for this to occur, you must make the time to become still and to know that you are God. You are God's spirit made manifest.

We have introduced you or opened you to receive the Hands of God. In the stillness those hands heal you from deep within. In the stillness those hands restore your soul and as is given in the *Course in Miracles,* all that is required is a little willingness on your part.

You cannot force your mind to change and you certainly cannot force your Heart and your emotions to change. You can, however, have the willingness to be changed, to be transformed and then it is up to the spirit of God, the hands of God to do the rest.

And there are some of you in this circle tonight, including this channel, who are experiencing that very process. Be still and know that I am God. The Healing hands of God wash away the illusions, the negativity that you take in as you walk the earth.

The healing hands of God embrace your mind and gently lift your mind out of illusions and into the reality of God where you know that God is present within you and present on the earth and very active in the lives of those who have said, "Yes."

Breathe God in this moment and let yourself be open and available and ready for miracles.

Let there be no barriers to your receiving the love God is always sending to you. When there are no barriers to your receiving the love God is always sending to you, then you are experiencing heaven on earth.

The barriers are always guilt and self-judgment. And guilt and self-judgment have no reason to be for you are the perfection of God made manifest.

Guilt and self-judgment have no reason to be, for I am the perfection of God made manifest. I will not judge myself for anything in any way. Thank you God. Praise God.

As you breathe, you open to receive and you allow the spirit of God the Hands of God to bring about the release and transformation you have called for. Allow yourself to be still and know the presence of God within you. Allow yourself to be still and know that you are God's spirit made manifest.

We want you to know, and honor and accept that your body is the creation of God and it is the temple of God's spirit. In your own mind and in your own Heart there needs to be a deep love and acceptance of your body.

Thank you God for opening me now to loving and accepting my body with all of my heart, all of my soul, all of my mind, all of my being, with all that I am. Thank you God.

We are happy to have this opportunity to work with you/ to serve you, to love you in this way once again. We want to speak with you for a few moments on the subject of free will.

You have the freedom on the earth to choose to receive the love and help and healing of God or to choose to shut yourself off from receiving it.

You have the freedom to think, to feel, to believe anything you choose to think, feel or believe. You have the freedom to do anything you want to do. You have the freedom to express yourself in anyway you choose to express yourself.

The experience of human beings on the earth has been an experience of souls who have chosen to live according to the free will of the ego self, to experience what it is like to live without consciously being guided by the spirit of God within. You each know that that choice causes confusion, pain, suffering, struggle and lack.

We have identified you as being the Higher Self of humanity, meaning you have long ago chosen to open consciously to the Spirit of God within and to have that part of you guide you, and through your experiences on the earth, heal and transform the parts of yourself, the parts of your soul which became caught or lost in pain, suffering, struggle, lack and darkness in the past.

What holds darkness together is guilt. So as you allow the Hands of God to touch you very deeply, the light, which emanates from those hands restores you to an awareness of your eternal innocence.

Now we identify you as being the Higher Self of humanity. You are in the minority on the earth. The majority of Souls on this planet are still choosing to be guided by the ego and have just begun to open to the spirit of God.

Whether or not you have been clear about this, the religions that have been created on the earth are a manifestation of just the slightest opening to the spirit of God. Therefore the teachings are confusing.

For there is light in the teachings, combined with the ego's will and stubborn need to hold on to a consciousness of separation.

You are here on the earth for the complete healing and transformation of your own souls, which allows you to open to the experience of enjoying everything. But you are also here to be ministers of God, to be channels of God's Light and Spirit in purity. The spirit you know as the Spirit of Jesus has had an ongoing communication with humanity on the earth.

Spiritual communication must break through the walls of

belief of the human ego self. Therefore spiritual truths have come through, but the human ego self has distorted them.

We say with great joy that in the last several years we have been able to reach souls who have attained a level of release of the ego through which the purest kind of teaching could come through.

We will speak now of one of those teachings and that is *A Course In Miracles*. That teaching is unambiguous. It presents the truth of God as being love and only love and it proclaims to humanity the fact that humanity, as one is the Holy Beloved Child of God.

Which is why we have brought through this channel the new ending to the Lord's Prayer: *For I am the Kingdom and the Power and the Glory forever and ever. Amen.* That is who and what you are.

We are speaking to you to encourage you to embody that even more and to accept that you are on the earth with souls who have not opened to the experience of God's truth as you have, souls who are very invested in separation. Yet on another level they are trying to learn what they need to learn to open to the light they need to open to, to have life as God wills it in overflowing abundance.

We will speak of a very sensitive subject now. One that has emotionally involved many as well as this channel.

We will speak of the elections, which were held recently in your country. The leadership is a manifestation of the collective consciousness of this country. And while you may be tempted to feel deeply discouraged and disheartened we want you to know that the light of God is moving. It is moving strongly on the earth, it is moving strongly through each of you. Therefore your leadership will not be static.

As you continue to grow and open, the collective consciousness must grow and open for you are a part of it. And therefore that leadership will grow and open no matter what form it is presently taking.

Nothing is stagnant now. Everything is moving. We will

work with each of you to help you process your own fear or pain or disappointment regarding this issue or any other life issue you may have. But please know that the light of God is moving on the earth.

You may need to be present and see others suffering because of choices they have made from their own free will. That is an essential part of their experience, that process of learning.

And you may go through periods where you feel brokenhearted over what you see. But as you allow the emotions to move, as you surrender your Heart to God, as you keep your Heart open to God's Holy Spirit the brokenheartedness is healed. All things can always be healed. All things can always be healed. All things can always be healed.

And breathe God in, knowing once again that you are here on the earth to enjoy everything this is why you were created by God, this is why you have life, this is your purpose and you are always completely supported by God in fulfilling your purpose.

Release into Unconditional Self Acceptance

Continue to breathe with the intention of love, of accepting all that you are, loving all that you are and receiving our love for you. You are here on the earth to heal your souls and to enjoy everything.

A major and important part of your spiritual practice is release. You are here on the earth to release the consciousness of pain, suffering, struggle and lack.

You are here on the earth to release anything and everything within you that is not presently manifesting in love and as love. You are here on the earth to enjoy everything: to enjoy being your Self, with a capital "S", to enjoy being who and what you are. You are here on the Earth to know that who and what you are is who and what you were created to be.

These are statements of truth and they are statements of love. These statements invite you, call you to stop struggling with yourself. They invite you, they call you, to stop rejecting yourself, to stop denying yourself. Who and what you are is who and what you were created to be. Breathe that into your Heart.

Thank you God for manifesting within me—and as me— right now.

Be still and know that I am God. As you breathe, you feel your God-Goddess self taking over within and around you.

We are encouraging you to live from your soul, to speak from your soul and to release from your soul. The soul is nonlinear, so as you release you may need to release something from five minutes ago or from five lifetimes ago.

Respect and honor yourself, your consciousness, what is going on within you and release what you need to release.

Unconditionally loving yourself is exactly what frees you from all pain, suffering and struggle. Loving all of yourself exactly as you are opens you to the consciousness and experience of Heaven on Earth. That means loving every thought, loving every feeling, loving every belief, loving every experience.

Now this opens a very deep question: Should you love the thoughts, feelings and beliefs that create pain and suffering and struggle?

You should love yourself as the creator, as the originator of every thought, feeling, belief and experience and it is through that love that total acceptance, that the thoughts, feelings, beliefs and perceptions that created pain and suffering and struggle are transformed. Your love of them heals and transforms them.

You perhaps cannot understand this at this time but as you meditate on it you will see how love is the key to freedom, to healing and to life. And the love for yourself cannot remain on the surface. You must love everything about yourself.

Your love for yourself must go to places within your soul, places within yourself that have never before received your love.

And as you breathe, you will receive love and you will receive an understanding of this teaching, of this truth on nonverbal levels. Praise God.

There are many things that are incapable of being expressed with words. It is the loving caress of God that communicates to you the love we are describing and all you need to know in order to be free from pain, struggle, suffering and lack.

We know that everyone who sits in this room this evening deeply and sincerely wants to be freed from pain, suffering, struggle and lack and so we are here to help you to accomplish this. To help you move into complete and total freedom and liberation.

And as we did in the Healing Prayer circle before this group, we ask you each to ask yourself—are pain, suffering, struggle and lack serving any purpose in your life and experience?

What you do not believe is serving a purpose, you will allow yourself to release and move beyond. Please say this prayer three times.

Pain, suffering, struggle and lack are serving no purpose in my life. I release them now from my mind, from my body, from my energy field and from my life—Thank you God.

Now you are here on the earth to enjoy everything, this is why you were created by God, this is your purpose and you are always completely supported by God in fulfilling your purpose.

Your spiritual, psychic abilities exist to help you to fulfill your purpose of enjoying everything. When you are fulfilled and in joy you add light to the wholeness of God, you add light to this creation and that is why God is deeply invested in your joy and in your fulfillment.

Introduction to and Teachings from Arc Angel Gabriel

I have done much work with Arc Angel Gabriel over the last eight years. I have experienced Gabriel in both masculine and feminine principle. She was the first Arc Angel I encountered and this happened quite spontaneously during an Advent Sunday Service I conducted in 1993. See my previous book, "*On Earth As It Is In Heaven.*

As I write these words I feel her presence and light and her deep love for us. She specializes in healing relationships and bringing us together with each other as well as music and all creative performing arts.

The Arc Angel Gabriel

My beloved siblings welcome to Heaven on earth. I welcome you now even if you have not yet attained the consciousness of Heaven on earth because I know you will. On the earth now you have everything you need to release pain, suffering, struggle and lack. You have everything you need in order to find God.

To find God you must of course look within. Keep looking do not stop your search until you find Her. This search requires some things from you. The search requires first and foremost that you be willing to feel what is within you. You must be willing to feel every emotion within.

This is not as easy as it may seem. You have all had a tendency to run away from feeling uncomfortable and painful emotions. We are asking you to feel your most uncomfortable and painful emotions and let them express and move through you. As you become accustomed to really allowing yourself to feel, you find that all emotions naturally want to flow through you and if you allow them to they always guide you back to peace, a feeling of inner peace.

Once you commit to this path of inner transformation all of the help in the universe is given to you. I do not need to repeat the lessons already brought forward in this book. My purpose is to make you aware of the Mother within you.

On the earth you are use to thinking of God as Father and that is why you have been so imbalanced. There is on the earth a huge denial of the Mother of Everything.

God is masculine and feminine and beyond both masculinity and femininity. Praise Goddess. The Mother within you is your capacity to feel. She is the emotional body within you. She is the key to your sexual freedom, your creative freedom. She is the key to your health and to your ability to love yourself and others.

Just breathe in the thought *"Mother God"* and see what it opens within you. It opens a whole part of your self and energy that has lain dormant, Praise Goddess. I guide you angels of God's Light to let yourselves be free. Let yourself leave the consciousness of this world—the established order and be the free beings you were created to be. You see that your established religions are based on half-truths and outright lies. Have the courage to let them go and follow Her word as it is revealed to you in your own heart.

We are with you we will always be with you. Continue to go within and ask for anything and everything you need. Do not make anything outside of yourself your spiritual authority. No teaching—no teacher, no channel, no minister, priest or rabbi etc. All of these things can be tools to open and guide you but are just tools meant to guide you to the teacher within and to strengthen your relationship with that teacher. Do not believe in the world. Believing in the world is very seductive because most of the people in the world believe in it.

And most of the people in the world are afraid, insecure, unbalanced, imbalanced, unhappy, unfulfilled, anxious, stressed, angry, etc. They have not opened to the will of God, which is love. They have not realized that they have the right and were created to love themselves with all of their heart, soul, mind, and being—with all that they are. I encourage you as brother Jesus did to be in the world but not of it.

Part 4

The Spirit of Jesus

Introduction

I, like so many people love Jesus deeply and consider him to be my main spiritual teacher.

My conscious relationship with him in this life did not come through Christianity but through the spiritual teaching *"A Course In Miracles"*. He is the voice and the source of the course.

He is our Elder Brother. He is my rock, my constant help in times of trouble. Praise God.

Rev. Daniel B. Neusom

Opening the Heart

In my conversations with you, I stress to you your Holiness, that all of life is Holy. I stress to you your purity, your innocence, your guiltlessness, your worthiness, your deservingness. And I send these messages to you over and over again so that they can reach the deepest layers of your consciousness and that is how you free yourself from suffering. And that is how the will of God is made manifest in your lives.

The will of God is for you to experience Heaven, always — for you to experience Heaven as you walk the earth.

As you know. Heaven is not a place you go to when you leave your body: Heaven is a state of consciousness. It is the consciousness of loving and accepting yourself unconditionally. It is the consciousness of knowing that you are without sin that you are without guilt, that you are wholly innocent.

There is great light being sent to this planet from the Heart of God. As this light works through you, wondrous miracles can happen within you and around you.

A miracle is a shift in your perception. It is a shift in your consciousness. This is the true meaning of *"Behold I make all things new."*

When you are born onto the earth in human form you bring with you an inheritance of illusion. Believing in your sinfulness, believing in your imperfection, believing in your lack, believing in your guilt. The work that we are doing is the work of dispelling, dissolving those beliefs, and bringing you back into an awareness of your truth: that you are the Holy, Beloved, Innocent, Creation of God, deserving of Heaven in every single moment. And I would like you to say that aloud:

> *I am the Holy, Beloved, Innocent, Creation of God, deserving of Heaven in every moment. I have no sin. I have no guilt. There is nothing I need to atone for. There are no karmic debts I must pay. I am free right here and right now.*

And breathe that in. With each breath, you will feel those of us who are your healing guides and friends working with your energy and opening you to receive.

Prayer is the act of accessing the power of God within you, using the power of your thought and your word to create.

The power of God within you, as you know, is the Holy Spirit. And we advocate the release of your illusion, the release of your burdens, the release of your pain to the Holy Spirit so that you can be made new in each moment.

We advocate your understanding and living according to the truth that your soul's purpose is found within your Heart. It is the fulfillment of your soul's purpose, the fulfillment of your Heart's desire. When you no longer believe in guilt you are in Heaven.

So I am going to ask you now to say a prayer of your own. Take a few moments to feel what you want to do with your freedom.

In the teaching we have given to the earth, *A Course in Miracle*, we tell you that you can never ask God for too much. Your problem is always in asking God for far too little.

In the prayer we have given through Daniel, we will tell you that you always deserve to receive everything, all the gifts of God, every gift, every blessing, every manifestation of God's grace. No matter what you say do, think, feel, believe or experience, it is impossible for you to ever be undeserving. No matter what you have said, done, thought, felt, believed or experienced, you always deserve to receive everything, all the gifts of God—every gift, every blessing, every manifestation of God's grace.

We encourage you to develop a more and more intimate relationship with God. Moving into your heart always and giving to God everything that is in the Heart. This is how you are healed and transformed on the deepest level of your being.

The Holy Spirit of God within you is the great healer, guide and transformer of your consciousness and your life. Our work is to guide you to a consciousness of unconditional self-acceptance and love.

And so we ask you to ask yourself today—how are you feeling about yourself? Am I loving myself today?

Look closely at the prayer: *I will not judge myself for anything in any way.* Being in that state of not judging yourself is being in Heaven. And our teaching is that there is never a reason for you to judge yourself for anything in anyway. You are always forgiven and there is nothing to forgive.

Pain and suffering and struggle are not natural for the spirit. And for the human self they have been the way of life. But the spirit within each human being is constantly seeking happiness and a way out of pain and suffering and struggle.

When you receive enlightenment, when God becomes a reality in you life, when Heaven becomes a reality in your life, you are confronted with the question:

Am I ready to go there? Am I ready to overcome the world? Am I ready to release my humanity?

And yet you are not releasing your humanity, you are redefining what it is to be human.

Am I ready to be a spiritual leader? Am I ready to open to a consciousness that is not known or understood, not the norm on the earth plane?

You want this or you would not be doing this work. You would not be reading this book if you were happy with staying in the consciousness of duality.

It is the support of God that gives you the courage to move forward and to overcome the world. And it is the support that you give to each other, those of you who are of like mind and on this path to Heaven together. You support each other in overcoming the world.

The earth plane, as you know, is very challenging because the majority, the vast majority, the overwhelming majority of people are unhealed. Every single person sends out an energy and co-creates the collective consciousness.

So you are here in the midst of that and you absorb it and that is why you must be vigilant, why you have to align yourself with God every day.

You must continue to strengthen that self-love which has grown so strong within you so that your energy is vibrating with a resounding "*Yes*"—vibrating with the truth:

Yes, I deserve to receive love.

As that grows stronger, the painful experiences will lessen and lessen and lessen. And you will get to a place where what had the power to hurt you in the past will not have the power to hurt you in the present Make yourself available to us so that light descends into you through your energy centers and releasing any pain or frustration or anger that has accumulated from your daily life experience. That is what strengthens you spiritually and your connection with spirit and your love for yourself.

I would encourage you to stop judging yourself for being selfish and to understand that the balanced way of life is to love yourself first.

And from that center of self-love, you love others. As your enlightenment deepens you begin to feel, not just in theory, but actually feel that we are not alone and that in loving yourself you are loving everyone. You are loving all of us.

You are in a process of transition now. Your consciousness is in transition from the consciousness of duality where your self-acceptance was entirely based on circumstances and events outside of yourself and you are moving into the consciousness of union where you know and accept yourself as the Holy Beloved Innocent child of God.

Now there are many illusions or conflicts held within the emotional body. The emotional body is the part of yourself that brings into manifestation what you experience. So when a painful thing happens to you, you are seeing reflected to you your own belief in guilt and lack that you are perhaps not conscious of. You can reach a place through your willingness to feel everything within you and to have Holy Spirit penetrate your consciousness so deeply that you will feel everything within you.

When something happens that is painful you will feel the cause within yourself: a recognition of *"Oh, this is a manifestation of my not really feeling worthy of what I'm calling for, what I say I want to have and experience.* Then you will not experience that split within; you will see that everything that is manifesting is a creation of your thoughts, feelings, beliefs and perceptions.

So the problem has been an unconsciousness. Do not judge this; understand it as natural. Most human beings are unaware of a large and essential part of their consciousness, the part that is creating their reality.

The collective consciousness of humanity is calling out for miracles now, for deep shifts in perception and deep awakenings. The collective human consciousness is calling out for the Spirit of God to make all things new, to create a new heaven and a new earth.

Do not look to the mind to solve the problems on the earth. The mind does not have the answers. The problems are meant to elevate humanity to a new level of consciousness, into the realm of spirit for spirit does have the answers.

The answer is the release of the ego consciousness: the belief in separation and the healing of the past so that you begin again with a clean slate, holding no judgments against yourself or each other. No grievances against self or others.

So join with us in saying this prayer for the healing of the collective consciousness and heart:

The light and power of God is making all things new within and around all of us now. The door to love is open.

Teaching From The Spirit of Jesus

My Beloved ones think for yourselves and trust your own logic, reason and experience. Our Creator's Light is continually being poured out unto the earth. As you are a part of Her, this Light is poured into your spirit. This is why it is difficult for you to continue to believe in the old images of God and of me.

My purpose now is to usher you into Heaven. Now, not later, but now. As you know I don't mean heaven after you die I mean heaven here on earth. In order for this to occur you must choose to be in your Heart and spirit and not in your ego.

I will once again define what your ego is. It is the need within you to appear other than what you are. It is the need to look good to others, to be special and superior. It is the desperate need to be loved and admired. This comes from hating yourself. This self-hatred has created war, slavery, prejudice, violence, sexism, homophobia, intolerance, pain, suffering, struggle and lack.

These things have been associated with God and the religion your egos have created in my name. I know how long you have believed in this reality and how hard you may find it to let it go and accept it as a lie of the devil. But take a look around you. Have these false teachings created a joyous balanced fulfilled life on this earth?

I am a teacher of love and acceptance and forgiveness. Is it logical to kill and hate and persecute others in my name? Is it logical to believe that unless you accept and receive me as your Lord and Savior you will burn in hell eternally? These have been believed to be the teachings of God and they are false.

Once again I will tell you the truth. You are the holy beloved child of God in whom God is always so very well pleased. You are always innocent, worthy and deserving. You have no sin, you have nothing to atone for, you have no karmic debts to pay and there is no price you ever have to pay for your life. In truth you are free right here and right now.

I ask you to consider the fact that you are free right here and right now. You can be in Heaven right here and right now. It isn't happening because you don't believe it. You don't believe it because you have been holding on to the old way of thinking and feeling for lifetimes. It is time to wake up if you choose. That's my task, to help you awaken if you choose. Praise God.

When you start to feel and think in the new way I am presenting, you will no longer hate yourself. And when you no longer hate yourself, you will not be internally destructive. When you are no longer internally destructive you will no longer be externally, physically, destructive. There will be peace on earth. There will be Heaven on earth: "Thy Kingdom come, Thy will be done on earth as it is in Heaven"

To achieve this you must practice. Go within and I will meet you and together we will journey to The Fathers House. Amen.

Releasing the Ego

I am guiding your path as you open to receive me. In your ego's many of you have a deep resistance to receiving me based on all of the distortions being presented as to who and what I am.

These teachings are calling you to move out of your ego and into your heart and real selves. This is not so easy to do.

I will begin by helping you to see how your ego works and how much you are in it. Do you believe one religion or spiritual path is superior to another? Do you believe that God has a chosen people? Do you believe God favors some people over others or loves some people more than others? Do you have a strong racial identity? Do you need to feel separate from other people? Do you need to feel superior to other people?

If your answer to any of those questions is "yes" it is your ego talking.

There is no judgment from God nor should there be from you about being in your ego. You will be in your ego for as long as you hunger for the experiences that being in your ego provides.

As you know, being in your ego does not give you peace of mind. It does not give you real security.

Being in your ego causes you to live in a state of fear and insecurity. You cannot know or experience God when you are in your ego.

It is possible and happens frequently that you move in and out of your ego during your incarnation and even during the course of a day.

When you are in your ego. You are not capable of receiving love.

The longer you experience life in your ego, the lonelier you become, and the more you long for love.

There is a certain point in the development of each entity when they can no longer bear the pain, fear and loneliness of ego.

When you reach that point, you begin to work consciously and seriously on your path to enlightenment. You then want to be and are willing to be out of ego.

The more you are out of ego the more you become aware of my presence within and around you.

I am your brother and I love you more than can be

expressed. My commitment to you is to guide you home to your center—to be in your real self.

I have no investment in whether you acknowledge or accept me consciously—but naturally as your ego dissolves, the blockages in our relationship dissolve and we join as one.

I am alive within and around you in complete support of your total healing and transformation and movement into the consciousness and experience of Heaven on earth.

My most essential teaching is the teaching of forgiveness. Forgiveness is letting go of grievances. It is accepting that every destructive thought, word, feeling, belief, action, perception and experience has been an essential part of yours and everyone else's development.

As you accept this you release your judgment, your anger, your resentment, your need to retaliate, your need for revenge and you allow the love of God to fully enter in and move you into the consciousness and experience of Heaven on earth.

You need only focus on forgiving yourself. For as you allow the Holy Spirit within you to open you to a consciousness of forgiveness. You are naturally able to forgive others.

You are always forgiven and there is nothing to forgive.

You have had false images of me and also false images of God. In truth God cannot be understood by man/woman. For your purpose, however, of releasing patterns and experiences of pain, suffering, struggle and lack and moving into the consciousness and experience of Heaven on Earth, please know that God is unconditional, loving acceptance.

God is the spirit that we all live and move and have our being within.

God requires nothing from you and wants for you that which you want for yourself, your total freedom, fulfillment and joy.

I have been asked to be the ending voice of this book because so many human beings believe in me and have developed a relationship with me.

You will only be able to relate to and accept this book as truth if you have had enough of being in the ego consciousness and all of the negative drama that being in the consciousness creates.

The majority of people who are in that consciousness are not ready to leave it. They have more experiences to be had and more lessons to be learned while in that consciousness.

You who are reading these words and resonating with them are ready to move but may have difficulty moving into heaven while so many of your siblings need to have more experience on earth or in hell on earth.

Join together beloved ones. Reach out to each other, support each other in overcoming the world.

You are the elder siblings of humanity. Your younger siblings will need you in the future. They will need you to be strong in your consciousness of freedom and unlimited deservingness so that you can point the way home for them when they are ready to return.

Be of good cheer for this world really is an illusion where you can come and live and die experience joy and pain, lack and abundance. Where you can be man and woman and child, where you can suffer and struggle and overcome and prove your worth and value to your selves and each other.

You have the right to be in the ego consciousness until you have received all of the expansion in your capacity to love that it can give you. Then it is time to come home.

When you return home you are much different than you were when you left. You've opened and grown in your capacity to love and create.

I love you with all of my heart, all of my soul, all of my mind, all of my being, with all that I am.

Thy kingdom has come Thy will is done on earth as it is in heaven.

Epilogue

It has been my pleasure to serve God and humanity as a minister for the past nineteen years. Nothing brings me more joy, than to see a person heal, transform and overcome by opening to the Spirit of God within and allowing that Spirit to teach and guide them.

As I write the concluding words of this book the words "All things are possible with God" come to mind.

We've heard those words but do we really believe them? All things are possible with God.

The spirit of the creator of heaven and earth lives within you. And as you allow that spirit to take over within you all things are possible.

My life on this path becomes more and more heavenly and I am so grateful to God and all of the angels She sends to help us.

I pray that you follow the call of God and allow yourself to walk the path to Heaven, the consciousness and experience of Heaven on earth.

This is an amazing and exciting time on the earth spiritually, God has sent to the earth and given us all we need to totally heal, transform and self realize.

If you choose, please say "*YES!*" to God and to yourself. Praise God.

Printed in Great Britain
by Amazon